Making Employer and University Partnerships Work

Making Employer and University Partnerships Work

accredited employer-led learning

Editors Bop Dhillon, Therese Edmonds,
Alison Felce, Ann Minton, Tony Wall

First published in 2011 by Libri Publishing

Copyright © Libri Publishing

Authors retain copyright of individual chapters.

ISBN 978 1 907471 49 0

A CIP catalogue record for this book is available from The British Library

Cover and text design by Carnegie Publishing

Printed in the UK by Short Run Press

Libri Publishing
Brunel House
Volunteer Way
Faringdon
Oxfordshire
SN7 7YR

Tel: +44 (0)845 873 3837

www.libripublishing.co.uk

Contents

Foreword

Partnerships between employers and universities have always been central to the work of the higher education sector. Many partnerships are founded in research and technology transfer, the processes of accreditation of employer-based training has led to a significant growth of new relationships based on learning and development.

The benefits to universities that derive from these partnerships are wide ranging. They include a strengthened reputation for employer engagement, actively addressing social mobility by providing opportunities for people in work who would not otherwise access higher education, opportunities for further progression, curriculum enhancement and income streams.

These partnerships also have a positive impact on the full time undergraduate provision. The transfer of knowledge from practitioners to academe enriches programmes through staff development, the use of contemporary case studies and relevance and currency of curriculum. At a time when employability and career destinations are increasingly important factors in selecting a course of study, evidence of strong employer partnerships will reinforce the value of the offer.

The benefits to employers and employees include external verification and enhancement of existing in company staff development programmes, clear opportunities for further progression, an injection of external expertise directly into the business that provides opportunities for employees to look beyond their immediate horizon and actively demonstrates a commitment to employee engagement supporting retention and recruitment strategies.

Foundation Degree Forward **fdf** has led the employment and higher education sectors in this area of activity through the Employer-based Training Accreditation Service (EBTA). First piloted in 2006 EBTA has developed over seventy new partnerships between employers and universities with accreditation at the heart of each new development. There are an estimated six thousand new higher education learning opportunities created as a consequence of these partnerships; importantly the majority of the partnerships will last many years providing ongoing opportunities for work based learners to access higher education.

*'The contribution of **fdf** to the process of facilitating the understanding between industry and the higher education sectors cannot be underestimated. Without **fdf** leading the way, bridging the gap between purely academic achievement and achievement within the workplace would be difficult if not impossible.'*

Dave Smith Murco Petroleum Limited

In parallel with the employer facing part of the EBTA service **fdf** established a small group of universities interested in exploring the complexities of accrediting employer training and developing partnerships. This group expanded to an enthusiastic Community of Practice with over 35 universities sharing knowledge and developing new practice in this field.

It therefore comes as no surprise to find this publication dedicated to Making Employer and University Partnerships Work. The book is grounded in practice with each chapter capturing and articulating the learning from specific partnerships and projects with contributors from industry and higher education. The first part of the book provides case studies that give a rounded perspective of the opportunities, obstacles and solutions to developing partnerships; the second part addresses issues of impact, relationships and quality.

As **fdf** hands over the leadership of this activity to the wider higher education community it is important to remember that partnership and collaboration will continue to be central to both employers and universities as they strive to strengthen the education and skills base of the UK workforce.

Charles Pickford Director of Employer Partnerships (Private Sector) **fdf**
Dave Smith Support Services Manager Murco Petroleum Limited

CHAPTER 1

Introduction

Bop Dhillon, Associate Director and Manager of the EBTA Service, *fdf*

'we will create the conditions to encourage greater collaboration between higher education institutions and employers to ensure that students gain the knowledge and skills they need to embark on rewarding careers.'

(BIS 2011, White Paper, para 32)

'The HE White Paper published today will: ...

- Encourage universities to engage actively with employers to accredit or "kitemark" courses to indicate to students that they are valued by them.'

(BIS 2011a, Press Release on White Paper)

The consistent message from government since the publication of the Leitch Review of Skills (2005) to the HE White Paper of June 2011 (above) has been the key importance of ensuring the availability of higher level skills needed for the future of the UK economy and society and for employers and universities to work in partnership to achieve this.

The Leitch Review (HM Treasury, 2006) set a target of 40% of the UK working population to be qualified at level 4 or above by 2020. Edmunds (Young and Garnett, 2007), formerly team leader of the DfES Skills Group suggested that traditional routes into HE may not be sufficient to achieve the Leitch target. Current demographic trends indicate that 70% of the 2020 working population have already left compulsory education (Young and Garnett, 2007) and so it is people who are already in the workplace who need to be the focus for developing our higher level skills base. This is emphasised by Department for Universities and Skills (DIUS) in its report *Higher Education at Work* (DIUS, 2008):

'Higher education providers must develop new ways of working if they are to meet the potential market from employers and employees.'

This has more recently been restated by John Hayes, Minister of State for Further Education, Skills and Lifelong Learning in his forward to the BIS consultation document 'Skills for Sustainable Growth (2010):

> 'We want to build a system driven by the informed choices of learners and employers. This means giving providers the flexibility they need to meet the needs of different learners and different economic sectors.'

UK plc has invested substantially in the upskilling of its workforce. The 2007 National Employer Skills Survey (NESS) calculated that UK plc invested £38.6 billion on workforce development. However, according to the HE Business and Community Survey 2006–07, HE accessed only £400 million of a potential £5 billion-worth of provision that HE could have delivered (Howat, 2008). Strengthening relationships with industry to support workforce development is a substantially untapped market for much of the HE sector, and hence has become a strategic priority for the Higher Education Funding Council for England (HEFCE).

A 2007 HEFCE circular made explicit the need for flexible provision, work based learning and accreditation of experiential learning as key development priorities for stimulating demand for HE products and services from industry. Both DIUS (2008) and the CBI (2008) identified HE accreditation of employer-based training, the current unique selling point of HE, as key to capturing greater share of this employer market.

Higher Education for the Workforce: Barriers and Facilitators to Employer Engagement (DIUS, 2008) and *Beyond Known Unknowns: A further exploration of the demand for higher level skills from businesses* (Kewin *et al*, 2009) detailed how HE must adapt its products, processes and services to enhance its appeal to industrial training markets in the context of Leitch targets for higher level skills. The latter made specific mention of the desire by employers to have their in-company training accredited.

Kewin et al (2009) emphasised that what the HE sector may perceive to be 'innovative' delivery methods come as standard in the private training sector, who are also able to operate from a lower cost base.

> It would be a high risk strategy for any HEI to attempt to compete with private training providers in the market for non-credit/non-qualification bearing short course training. HEIs must play to their strengths and exploit their unique selling point.
> (Kewin *et al.* (2009) p.41)

Employer-based Training Accreditation (EBTA) – A Response

In the context of the above, the EBTA Service has represented a significant response to HEFCE priorities for strengthening the higher education (HE) sector's relationship with industry, to meet the current and future skills needs of UK plc. Over the 6 years of its existence the EBTA Service has offered a highly valued independent and impartial approach to building relationships between employers and universities to provide accreditation. Having originally started out as a pilot in the North West of England in 2006–07, the last three years has seen the EBTA Service evolve into a robust mainstream service for both employers and the higher education sector.

In the government consultation document, 'Higher Education at Work', EBTA was specifically referenced as an exemplar model of higher education engagement with industry '...We are learning from the early experience of **fdf**'s Employer-based Training Accreditation scheme and accreditation of in-house provision is specifically included in a number of the employer engagement projects HEFCE is funding or expects to fund' (DIUS, 2008)

This message was reinforced at the official launch of the EBTA service in the House of Commons in 2008 by Kelvin Hopkins (MP, Chair of the All Party Parliamentary Group on Further Education) who commented: 'EBTA will encourage employers to recognise the importance of improving the skills of their workforce and applies the rigorous standards of university learning to their in-house provision'

In one of the first articles about EBTA to appear in the **fdf** journal 'Forward', Sharpe (2008) wrote that in building upon the successful pilot phase, '**fdf** will be seeking to capitalise on progress made during the developmental phase to ensure the scheme is firmly established as a major and permanent contributor to raising higher level skills in the workplace' and that within this context, higher education providers would come to view accreditation as the key starting point for developing and expanding a dialogue with employers about work based higher education (Sharpe, 2008).

EBTA has worked with over 200 employers such as Booths, HMRC, The Treasury, Q Hotels, Murco Petroleum, and The Fire Protection Association resulting in the formation of 69 employer-HE partnerships.

Current Context – Accreditation Growing in Significance

Through EBTA, accreditation of in-company training has been seen as a valuable first step towards the development of partnerships between employers and universities based upon employer learning and development strategies. Strengthening such activity will have increased relevance for many Higher Education Institutions (HEIs), particularly in the new era of higher education funding, which will necessitate employers reviewing their arrangements for workforce development and graduate recruitment and development. Employers will be seeking closer working relationships with higher education partners and will wish to support new and innovative approaches to curriculum development and delivery to support the development of higher levels skills in the workplace. Browne in the recently published review of future funding for higher education located accreditation of employer in-company training increasing in significance of recognition for learning and experience in the workplace and stimulating demand for further, lifelong learning.

'There is also an increasing number of employers who work with institutions to accredit skills developed in work to count towards a degree programme. This can provide an important 'second chance' for people who missed out on higher education after school to acquire a degree later in life and it can provide re-training in new skills – increasingly important in a changing economy. The HE Council may invest in ensuring that such accreditation is happening in all regions and all sectors of the economy' (Browne Review 2010, p.54)

The EBTA Community of Practice – Responding to the Challenges Posed by Accreditation

Robust yet efficient mechanisms for quality assuring higher level learning derived from outside of the institution has historically remained problematic across the university sector. Acknowledging these challenges, the EBTA community of practice has provided a forum for universities to share experience and expertise to strengthen their own respective institutional systems and processes, and to support a growing strategic emphasis upon employer partnerships.

The EBTA Service has built up a network of 37 universities which have all signed a Memorandum of Understanding to be represented within an EBTA 'Community of Practice'. The network reflects the full range of diversity across the HE sector, a mix of pre- and post-'92 institutions. In the case of many post-'92 institutions, whose traditions have been rooted in the delivery of flexible vocational higher education to non-traditional mature HE learners, employer engagement remains core to their institutional missions and strategies. For many pre-'92 institutions there is an acknowledgement that employer engagement is perhaps a more marginal activity but yet growing in significance.

At the first Community of Practice event focusing upon Quality, Stephen Jackson of the Quality Assurance Agency for Higher Education (QAA) emphasised that the UK has a long history of inclusive applied learning and high regarded provision with a mix of theory and practice provided regardless of venue, preparing learners using appropriate models of high value learning.

Hardacre and Workman (2010) also emphasise that whilst the concept of work based learning is well established across the education sector, within the higher education context it has tended to remain a relatively marginal activity. The discourse around work based learning has however gained momentum alongside the emergence of Foundation Degrees, within which work based learning reflects a core characteristic differentiating this HE qualification from equivalent HND's, and a growing policy and strategic emphasis upon employer engagement.

For a time, the HE community grappled to gain clarity and consensus regarding accepted definitions of work based learning. Much of the work based learning literature has made consistent reference to the definition of work based learning as 'learning that takes place for, in, and through paid and unpaid work' Universities Association for Lifelong Learning (UALL, 2006) and it is this definition that reflects approaches to work based learning throughout this text. Quite deliberately referring to 'approaches' to work based learning in the plural rather than singular, the contributions to this publication reflect examples of work based learning along a 'continuum', ranging from accreditation of prior experiential learning (APEL), accreditation of in-company training, through to bite sized CPD provision and the provision of full HE awards through part-time access.

This sentiment of a 'continuum' is reflected in the 'Ladder of Accreditation' that has come to be associated with EBTA (see Figure 1.1). This continuum attempts to unravel the complexity of the broad term 'accreditation' into a number of discrete practical outcomes. In this context the following guiding principles reflect good practice in accreditation of in-company training within the context of EBTA:

- Demonstrating innovation and creativity in interpreting QA procedures
- Being responsive and flexible
- Prioritising the needs of employers and employees
- Empowering employers
- Focuses upon outcomes rather than inputs
- Aiming to achieve maximum accreditation possible
- Facilitating progression and lifelong learning

Figure 1.1: The ladder of accreditation

Ladder of accreditation: descriptors	
Forms	**Descriptors**
1. **Approval for training to be recognised for a university qualification. (For example, University Certificate, Foundation degree, Postgraduate Diploma)**	The HEI approves employer-based training for named qualifications from the HEI concerned. Awards might range from a one module certificate to a full Foundation degree or honours degree or postgraduate qualification. The level of engagement required will probably limit this to larger employers with a sufficient volume of employees and 'repeatable business' to justify costs. It is assumed (unlike form 4 below) that this will need to undergo a full validation procedure.
2. **Learning through work/CPD/ professional development shell awards**	The HEI matches the employer-based training to an existing award set up as a 'shell' for the 'student' to negotiate the relevant content and/or learning outcomes. These have been set up by a number of HEIs and are often referred to as learning through work awards, or continuing professional development (CPD) Frameworks. Employees are enrolled either individually or in groups, funded either by the employee or the employer. In some cases, HEIs have approved 'shell modules' that relate more to credit recognition.
3. **Credit recognition (specific credits)**	**Specific** credit is applied where there is a direct match between the content and learning outcomes of the external course and existing provision offered by a university so that the individual given the credit is agreed to have gained a similar study experience. These credits are then available to the employee for progression to higher education (HE) awards: either clearly specified in the credit recognition process; or used more generally through the accreditation of prior learning (APL). In the latter case training is not recognised as a direct match with the learning but the experience is none the less seen as a recognised benefit to the course and so the learning credits are used to enter or progress on the course.
4. **Credit recognition (general credits)**	The HEI recognises training provided by the employer as equivalent to a specified number of HE credits at an agreed level. **General** credit refers to the academic level at which the external course is assessed and are not directly matched against any existing provision by a university (in contrast to specific credits above). These credits are then available to the employee for progression to HE awards: either clearly specified in the credit recognition process; or through APL.
5. **Articulation agreements**	The HEI enters into an agreement with an employer whereby employees who have undertaken an agreed programme of employer-based training will be eligible for admission to a specific programme of study at the HEI, either at the start of the programme or part-way through.

Ladder of accreditation: descriptors	
6. **Accreditation of prior (experience and) learning (APL or APEL)**	Employers are asked to make their employees aware that on the basis of the training undertaken, they may be able to gain APL from a named HEI which will provide exemption from part of an existing award of the HEI.
7. **Kite marking or endorsement** (See Chapter 20 for a discussion on this form of accreditation – referred to there as Recognition)	The employer or training provider pays an HEI to endorse a programme of training. That is the HEI acknowledges that the training is at an HE level but no credits, specific level, or awards specified. The *fdf* Endorsement Service can be seen as an example of this. The latter is clearly about quality *enhancement* rather than quality *assurance*.

(Taken from the revised EBTA Guidance Manual for HEIs, 2010)

Aims and Objectives of this Publication

A key objective within the Memorandum of Understanding to which all members of the EBTA Community of Practice subscribed was to:

'develop and publish the results of their EBTA initiatives for the higher education sector and carry out evaluation and research, with support from **fdf.'**

This publication is a significant and substantial outcome of that commitment.

This publication is aimed at HE strategists, policy makers, managers, educational practitioners and academics with an interest in employer engagement and employer responsive provision, and for extending HE opportunities to those in work and the contribution that universities can make to the wider higher level skills agenda. It adds to and complements the growing contemporary literature that brings together the full breadth of theory and practice that has until recently been lacking.

We have purposefully tried to ensure that the language and terminology used throughout this text enables the publication to be equally accessible to HR and learning and development practitioners in industry, colleagues within employer representative and professional bodies and trade union activities engaged in the learning agenda. The majority of the case studies presented in Part One are also jointly authored between an employer and a university colleague. It has often been cited by industry that higher education speaks a different and often jargonistic language and so this publication endeavours to offer a bridge between the worlds of academia and learning and development within an industry context.

The principle focus of this publication is how universities can support and enhance learning at level 4 and above that is being undertaken in the workplace, and particularly learning that is provided directly by employers rather than by the universities themselves. Not all of the chapters are based upon EBTA initiatives specifically but the totality of institutional experience has impacted greatly upon institutional approaches, processes and practices as reflected throughout this text.

Structure of the Book

The publication is essentially in two parts.

Part 1 consists of case studies of employer-university partnerships supporting employer-based learning and these have been co-authored by business and university colleagues. In many cases, case studies reflect an action learning approach to the opportunities, issues and challenges associated with integrating the 'guiding principles' underpinning good practice in accreditation of in-company training within the context of the EBTA service as listed above.

Part two examines some substantive themes that have emerged from practice, especially in relation to quality assurance processes, and the beneficial impact resulting from employers and universities working together in genuine partnership.

There is a substantial amount of reinforcement of key issues across the case studies which form part 1 as would be expected, which are then explored more fully in part 2. As such, a thematic approach to the introduction and overview of chapters within this publication has been adopted, under the overarching headings of Impact, Relationships and The Academic Infrastructure and Quality Assurance.

Overview of the Book: The Theme of Impact

Chapter 5 explores specifically the limitations in realising Return on Investment (ROI) in the context of HE programmes which perhaps extend over longer timeframes through an overview of the development of a bespoke Diamond Professional Graduate Certificate Programme (DDP) as a core component of DeBeers UK talent strategy. The DDP was delivered to a global learner cohort via a blended learning approach over the course of one year. The ROI impact study found that to recoup the total investment in the programme, resultant impact must be driven for two to three years post programme, highlighting the longer term nature of talent development programmes.

Chapter 6, 'Journey in Practice' looks at accreditation at the heart of an organisational change and development programme within Halifax Community Bank. The case study provides an overview of how negotiated work based projects linked to business activity opened learners eyes to the benefits of reflection in their work, motivating the development of behaviours across the workforce that drove the business forward. In a context of change, the ROI resulting from accreditation was clear as key business metrics such as service standards and sales targets were exceeded and team working was strengthened. The inclusion of a work based project was also instrumental in demonstrating application and ROI of Booths store manager training as outlined in Chapter 2. Chapter 9 similarly demonstrates how the introduction of a work based learning module proved to be a powerful vehicle for assessing the effectiveness of an in-house programme, evidencing embedding of community cohesion training in practice.

The value of work based learning is in the realisation of its relevance for individuals and Chapter 12 quotes Knowles (1990): 'Adults pursue learning that can be applied immediately'. This chapter draws close parallels to Chapter 10 which discusses the impact of a training intervention in partnership with P&O, covering a diverse workforce operating across all levels. Both case studies outline the importance of developing leaders first as a necessary precursor to moving towards becoming learning organisations. Specifically the case study of P&O is considered in the context of the majority of managers having no formal management training or qualifications and apprehensive about the prospect of engaging in learning again for fear of failure. Success derived from understanding the diversity of the learner population and adapting approaches to introducing learning accordingly.

Chapter 9 provides a case study of engendering positive attitudes towards independent learning and reflective practice, strengthening the culture of CPD and career aspiration.

Chapter 14 explores the question that if an employer's in-company training is robust and works does HE accreditation actually add value, particularly if it creates an additional burden of assessment. In this context, the Phillips Return on Investment (ROI) model, grounded in Donald Kirkpatrick's 4 levels of training evaluation is considered as a useful framework for assessment design, strengthening the connection between learning and alignment to business needs, such that the impact of training can be more explicitly articulated and demonstrated. As such, accreditation can offer a convergence of the value of academic credit for both the employer and HEI in quantifying what is learned.

Overview of the Book: The Theme of Relationships

Looking backwards from the thematic chapters in part 2 to the case studies in part 1, Chapter 15 draws upon the collective experiences of Higher Level Skills Advisers appointed as part of an initiative by West Yorkshire Lifelong Learning Network

(WYLLN) in response to apparent problems encountered by employers engaging with the HE sector. The chapter draws some important conclusions for HEIs which are picked up across a number of case studies in part one, specifically relating to agility in response and proportionality in the application of HE systems and processes perceived by employers to be bureaucratic, and which ultimately have a bearing upon cost.

WYLLN developed the capabilities to deliver the EBTA service through its Higher Level Skills Advisers on behalf of its FE and HE partners. In Chapter 13, the case study 'Winning Moves – Winning Managers' is presented which arose out of a regional EBTA competitive tendering process and explores the rationale and principles associated with a partnership with a private training provider. It explores the partnership journey and considers the issues, opportunities and lessons learned. The case study parallels those presented in Chapters 7 and 8 demonstrating the types of innovative and powerful collaborations that can be achieved when committed stakeholders with a shared ethos and complimentary objectives work together to leverage mutual benefit deriving from the respective strengths of each other. In Chapter 7 for example, both organisations shared a philosophy about the importance of personal transformation achieved through experiential and work based learning.

The case studies in Chapters 7 and 13 are particularly interesting in their approaches to managing the duality of dilemmas associated with the competition-collaboration paradox inherent in partnerships which involve accreditation of the training programmes of private training providers. Both institutions viewed these partnerships as key opportunities to access more fragmented markets such as SMEs, community and voluntary sectors and to reach potential clients traditionally difficult for HEIs to engage.

Chapter 3 offers a related albeit alternative dimension to the benefits leveraged by the University of Gloucester through its partnership with the Cathedrals Workshop Fellowship. The very niche nature of the training for Cathedral Stonemasons enabled the university to develop a qualification which they may not otherwise have done given the complexities associated with the very small and geographically dispersed nature of the learners and consequent issues of viability and sustainability.

Chapters 2, 3, 4, 6 and 12 in their coverage of the partnership journey from both the perspectives of the employer and HEI, emphasise that true partnerships based upon trust and mutual understanding are built from a recognition of the expectations of each in respect of standards, contexts, terminology, timeframes and ethics. Chapter 4 discusses the development of the relationship between the University of Derby and Croda International leading to accreditation of their New Manager Programme. Specifically it discusses the challenges associated with balancing business timeframes, adept at quickly translating business proposals into reality and benefits, with academic processes. It also considers the issues of the potential risk for both organisations. Chapters 2 and 6 both emphasise the need to demystify HE language and terminology and identify a shared language to facilitate communication creating a context to develop shared understanding. Chapter 12 discusses the imperatives for HEIs to work flexibly and innovatively, often within a context of competing pressures and constraints, and also emphasises the importance of a 'Plan, do review' approach to ensure that provision remains current and continues to meet business need within the fast paced Event Safety Management industry.

Consistently referred to as key to linking a strong partnership approach to optimising benefits realisation from accreditation and work based learning, has been the HEI input into strengthening the capability and capacity within the organisation to support work based learning. This also links more fundamentally to the issues and challenges associated with the Universities role in assuring the quality of provision delivered outside of the confines of the institution and by employers themselves. Implications for the Cathedrals Workshop Fellowship delivering a programme in the absence of a training department or experience of co-ordinating training across the organisation are discussed in Chapter 3. A number of other case studies refer to supporting employers with the development of internal coaches within the organisation and of delivering 'Train the Trainer' programmes such that over time, the employers themselves may take on greater ownership of the accredited programme including assessment and internal moderation. Chapter 4 refers to 'Supporting Work Based Learning in HE', itself an accredited programme developed by the University of Derby as the basis for a 'Community of Practice' of work based trainers responsible for accredited work based programmes within their organisations, providing a valuable vehicle for sharing and developing practice in this area.

The above approaches pre-suppose a light touch intervention by institutions in supporting higher level learning within organisations. However, it is important to acknowledge that levels of HE involvement in delivering employer-led curriculum extends across a continuum from moving towards light touch intervention, to quite high levels of HE intervention. An example of the latter is presented in Chapter 11 which reflected an innovation in HE-industry collaboration at the point of inception in 1989, but which has stood the test of time and which has stimulated a range of new developments in meeting the needs of the pharmaceutical manufacturing sector. The strong commitment of key employers and industry bodies in behind learning products that truly meet their needs has resulted also in stepwise growth which has made the provision self sustaining and is now being expanded into global markets.

Overview of the Book: The Themes of the Academic Infrastructure and Quality Assurance

This theme emerges very strongly in Part 2 of the book. Chapter 16 considers the QAA academic infrastructure and discusses the rationale for further articulation to clarify its application in the context of employer-based provision. It considers the variety of quality assurance challenges, aspects of the academic infrastructure in this context and the potential incompatibilities between employer and HE quality assurance expectations. The chapter suggests that whilst in some cases the existing academic infrastructure remains appropriate in others it can be synonymous with 'a sledgehammer to crack a nut' (Haddleton, 2011). In suggesting that risk based approaches to partner approval remain under-developed in awarding institutions, greater proportionality of approach that more appropriately reflect scales of risk, linked particularly to size and level of award should be adopted. These should be linked to but adapted from existing university systems. Chapters 18 and 19 compliment this overview by providing case studies from Harper Adams University and the University of Wolverhampton.

Chapter 18 emphasises that employer responsive provision is no different from any other HE provision in its requirement for robust quality assurance mechanisms to safeguard academic standards. It outlines Harper Adams University approach to developing proportionate approaches to the various aspects of the academic infrastructure, which draw upon the QAA Code of Practice as reference points or 'Anchors' in resolving emergent challenges, yet creating the context for deep learning and debate as the basis for creativity and innovation in developing responsive practices going forward. Chapter 19 outlines 'FLOW' which demonstrates how the university can remain responsive to market demand whilst ensuring university oversight of academic quality and standards. As an example of new processes but which align with existing university systems, FLOW is an example of 'Not reinventing the wheel but re-shaping it for a different need'. Both case studies demonstrate the application of many of the good practice recommendations emerging from demonstrator projects considered in Chapter 16.

Chapter 17 explores the wide ranging use of level descriptors within a work based learning context and which service as key reference points (within the context of the FHEQ) from which to map in-company learning programmes. It considers the role of level indicators to support development of shared understandings and benchmarking of learning and achievement and to clarify assessment expectations across a range of learning contexts. Specifically, this chapter considers the difference between regulatory and facilitative applications of level descriptors, emphasising that work based learning tends to be process driven rather than product based. Curriculum design, therefore, is output rather than input driven. As such, the tendency to stick rigidly to regulatory frameworks limits innovation and creativity of the individual learning journey whereas a facilitative framework recognises achievement which is equitable. There are close links between this chapter and Chapter 16 which considers the increasing use of shell award frameworks, pre-approved generic learning outcomes and short course module descriptors to allow flexibility in the application to a range of work based contexts, in turn enabling greater flexibility and efficiency in delivery of employer responsive provision, and allowing for the integration of employer in-company training programmes. Useful insights can also be drawn when this chapter is read in conjunction with Chapter 8 which considers the challenges associated with levelling corporate training programmes in ways that motivate and enhance learner performance and respond effectively to the expectations of employers.

The concept of 'Recognition' in contrast to 'Accreditation' is considered in Chapter 20. The chapter derives from research across ten EBTA Community of Practice institutions, acknowledging that whilst many institutions have considered offering 'Recognition' of an employers in-company training as equivalent to HE standards without conferring academic credit, the majority of institutions have chosen not to offer it. The chapter explores the issues associated with perceived reputational risk, challenges in developing robust yet proportionate approaches to recognition as distinct from accreditation, lack of awareness of potential demand and the absence of a compelling case of the potential benefits for engaging in this activity which outweigh the costs and risks. Chapter 20 presents an extremely interesting juxtaposition against the discussion around proportionality in Chapter 16.

The concluding chapter provides a conclusive overview to the 'Issues, Challenges and Joys of Accreditation'. It explores accreditation within the context of institutional strategy, emphasising the need for strategic level commitment to drive new and innovative ways of working cross institutionally as a pre-requisite for making accreditation work. Chapter 21 then provides an operational route map navigating through the complexity of university systems and processes to successful accreditation practices and finally considers the challenges for institutions in developing the internal capabilities to become more 'business facing' to support the establishment of strong HE-industry partnerships and to nurture those into sustainable and fruitful relationships going forward.

This text is testimony to the fact that the EBTA Community of Practice has pushed the boundaries of rhetoric and been creative and innovative amidst the array of challenges to traditional HE practice presented by the employer engagement agenda. We hope that in reading this contemporary contribution to the work based learning domain, you are equally inspired to test the boundaries within your own organisations to leverage the full range of benefits that can be realised through university partnerships with industry.

References

BIS, 2010, 'Skills for Sustainable Growth'

BIS, 2011, White Paper, Putting students at the heart of higher education, 28 Jun 2011

BIS 2011a, Press Release on White Paper, http://www.bis.gov.uk/news/topstories/2011/Jun/ he-white-paper-students-at-the-heart-of-the-system (accessed 30th June 2011)

Dhillon, B. & Phillips, K. (2010) 'EBTA Guidance Manual for HEIs', *fdf*

Hardacre, K. & Workman, B. (2010). Planning and Reviewing Work-based Learning: a practical guide. Learning and Teaching in Higher Education, Issue 4–2

HEFCE (2007). Allocation of additional student numbers in 2008–09 for employer engagement, circular letter number 03/2007, www.hefce.ac.uk/pubs/circlets/2007/cl03_07

Independent Review of Higher Education Funding and Student Finance (2010). Securing a Sustainable Future for Higher Education: An Independent Review of Higher Education Funding & Student Finance. Available at: www.independent.gov.uk/browne-report

Kewin, J, Bowes, L and Hughes, T (2009) Beyond Known Unknowns: A Further Exploration of the Demand for Higher Level Skills from Businesses, Leicester: CFE.

Sharp, J (2008). EBTA's rise to prominence since House of Commons Launch, Forward 16, 12–14. Available at: www.*fdf*.ac.uk

Young, G and Garnett, J (Eds) (2007). Work Based Learning Futures. Bolton: UVAC.

Leitch Review (HM Treasury, 2006). Prosperity for all in the global economy – world class skills. London, HMSO.

CHAPTER 2

Booths – the Journey from Retail Management Programme to Foundation Degree to Collaborative Partnership

Therese Edmonds, Training Manager, E.H. Booth & Co. Ltd

Steve Bainbridge, Manchester Metropolitan University

Executive Summary

Based in the North West, Booths, voted second best food and drink retailer in the world by *The Grocer* magazine, has 26 stores supported by a central, fresh food manufacturing and ambient distribution centre. The founder's philosophy: was to sell the best goods he could buy in shops staffed with first class assistants and this remains at the core of the company's values and how it trades. To this end, the business seeks to have embedded, structured training programmes that align to industry standards, in order to develop staff to their full potential in the ongoing quest to be the 'best' food and drink retailer.

Manchester Metropolitan University Business School (MMUBS) has a long-standing reputation for teaching and research excellence in retailing through the work of its Marketing and Retailing department. Recent developments had included a work based Foundation Degree (FD) in Retailing enabling employees of retail companies to undertake higher education learning and training in the work place.

Booths worked with the University to align the needs of its internal management training programme (MDP) in relation to their FD in Retailing. As a result, the

Booths MDP became accredited against the FD resulting in Booths trainee managers being able to undertake the MDP, followed by the remaining units of study of the FD to fully achieve Booths management training requirements and in so doing obtain a university qualification, the FD in Retailing. The key to this accomplishment was the ability of partners from industry and higher education to understand each other's objectives, priorities and abilities and work together towards a common goal.

This case study highlights the following:

- The rationale for seeking a Higher Education Institute (HEI) qualification
- The role of the retail manager in the context of the development
- Negotiating the adaptations from in-house Management Development Programme (MDP) to a link with Foundation Degree (FD) at the same time retaining unique business requirements and needs – in a speedy manner
- Stakeholder relationships and understandings and their importance in the development of work based learning programmes and future developments
- Strategic alignment of the partner organisations goals
- Evaluation of an in-house training programme in order to develop a collaborative partnership and the challenges of the move
- The potential mutual benefit of industry and higher education partnerships

Introduction

In its fifth generation, Booths is a family owned business who for its 163 years has embraced the 'human touch' within its business values. Booths aim to stay special by celebrating being 'Northern' and sourcing its products locally wherever possible. It intends to grow organically by caring for its customers, staff and next generation of leaders (see Booths website www.booths-supermarkets.co.uk/about-us). Over 80% of the current store management team started their career within the organisation either on a part time basis whilst still in education or as a general sales assistant. This is a real accolade to career development within the organisation, albeit previously unstructured, but can give rise to a much internalised view of retail. A clear early requirement was a structured career development path with opportunities for external influence where appropriate. And so the journey begins. As a member of the Sector Skills Council for Retail (Skillsmart), there was early awareness of the foundation degree and an opportunity to input into its content and ensure it was fit for purpose for Small and Medium Employers (SME) as well as the large employers. The timing of this aligned to the completion, for some of our management team, of a new internal Management Development Programme (MDP) and a natural progression and opportunity to gain higher level learning via external input where appropriate. As the Training Manager (TM) for Booths this was a first encounter of the challenges of learning a new language within the academic world and realising that the pace of business can be vastly different to that of the academic world. The TM met with two HEI's in the first quarter of a year and wanted to enrol the first cohort onto what was at the time a new programme at the next intake, namely September of the same year and also wanted completion of Booths in-house materials to be recognised and accredited. It was important that the HE partner could provide delivery of the programme that would embrace Booths unique trading style in a way that would allow a link back to the business culture and position within the industry whilst at the same time allowing synergy with the core values of the business. Rapid response by the HEI and ability to work to a timetable driven by Booths would also be a key factor in partner selection. The relationship between the TM at Booths and the key contact of the chosen HEI would also be instrumental in achieving this goal and indeed has been.

The company's culture is not to de-skill retail managers by strengthening the power of its central functions, but rather to retain retail store managers as effective general managers. They are expected to ensure individual stores operate within the context of the company's overall strategies and policies, but are also positioned in relation to their local market place. At least 25% of the company's product range is sourced locally. The company introduced a retail management development programme some five years ago. The programme is organised into three phases. Collectively the programme offers a development programme, enabling an individual to progressively move from new management trainee, to trained assistant manager to trained manager, as their skills develop and opportunities arise. The programme is strongly focused around work based learning supported by, for example, study guides, workbooks, company workshops, further reading, assessments and a personal development plan.

The company had two main strategic drivers in looking to work with an HE partner to assist with the accreditation and development of its MDP. These were:

1. To enable managers successfully completing the company's MDP to gain external recognition of their learning

2. To provide an opportunity to broaden the knowledge and understanding of the company's management team going forward via external input

Selecting an HE Partner

Compared with most businesses Booths enjoys very high retention rates in terms of its managers. As a result the company was keen to ensure its employees gained further opportunities for Continuing Professional Development (CPD) to up-date and extend their knowledge and enable them to become more knowledgeable and confident in putting forward new ways of running and developing the business. Increased networking with other partners in this programme was also seen as a business advantage.

It was important that the costs of the programme were affordable and this was to be achieved by minimising the impact on the business as follows:

- Ensuring periods of study release were kept to a minimum
- Seek to avoid using periods when retail sales are expected to be high for major elements of learning or assessment
- Expecting individuals to study in their own time
- Maximising the number of units for which accreditation was sought e.g. 120 credits

A further consideration was to deliver units within the business where appropriate. (To this end, the Managing Information unit is currently co-delivered by the Booths IT Director) This change highlighted the need to be clear about outcomes and goals for the cohort and to understand where challenge is appropriate.

The Manchester Metropolitan University (MMU) programme was selected by the company on the basis of the following:

- It was one of only two work based learning national foundation degrees in retailing
- The delivery team was judged to have a strong and relevant retail knowledge base
- The MMU representatives demonstrated an understanding of Booths priorities and a willingness to work flexibly to achieve them
- The close geographical proximity of the University to the Company's Central Office and many of its stores

Developing the Partnership

Notwithstanding the decision in principle to move forward with MMU, there were a number of fundamental items of detail that needed to be clarified, namely:

- Was the programme full or part-time?

- The length of time students were expected to take to complete the programme

- Attendance pattern: how much work could be done on-line or remotely and to what extent would students be expected to be involved in face-to-face sessions?

- To what extent would the University units differ from those completed as part of the MDP? How might these differences be presented and managed bearing in mind students' expectations?

- What level of student support would be provided? (By both parties)

- To what extent could elements of the University programme be customised?

Booths entered into dialogue with MMU in July 2008. An independent evaluation by an **fdf** EBTA consultant suggested that the company's MDP might be worth the equivalent of 80 credits of the FD. The initial signposting indicated by the independent evaluation was subsequently used by the University course team to map units of the Booths MDP to units of the FD. The first cohort of students from Booths was admitted to the MMU FD in Retailing in September 2008. These applicants were admitted to the programme with advanced standing of 80 credits based on the Accreditation of Prior and Experiential Learning (APEL).

Subsequent work by Booths supported by **fdf** during 2008–09 led to a further enhancement of the MDP, including the introduction of new learning materials to enable a company-based project to be included in the accreditation. The enhancement now allows cohorts from Booths to gain additional advanced standing (subject to successful assessment supervised by MMU), increasing the total to 120 credits. The positioning of a work based project which has to ultimately be delivered to the board of directors ensures the emphasis of this work based programme has a more measurable return on investment to the business.

The philosophy of the MDP of Booths and that of the MMU's FD programme in retailing are closely aligned.

'The programmes have a strong practical and vocational focus. In particular Stage 3 of the management programme allows participants to consider specific retail situations and to reflect on their wider applicability.' (Booths, Guide to Management

Development Programmes: an overview, p.2). Similarly, the philosophy of the MMU FD in Retailing is 'intended to be vocationally oriented, contain a high degree of work based learning and be focused upon the achievement of employer specific needs.' Additional it states 'students will be able to propose creative yet practical solutions to complex problems within a retail management context, and make appropriate and effective management decisions within a retail business.' (MMU Business School, Foundation Degree in Retailing Student Handbook, p.7).

Over the last two years an increasingly close working relationship has developed between MMU and Booths. The period since 2008 has seen the company and MMU sharing public platforms and jointly supporting other retail companies on how they might mirror the partnership built between the company and the University. For example, the Booths/MMU partnership was featured at the industry workshop, *Improving Business Performance through Skills,* which was held on the 10th September 2009 at the Grosvenor House Hotel, London.

Further, MMU has asked Booths on occasions to speak privately to other national retailers when these companies have been exploring the accreditation of their programmes. Booths have been able to provide insights to other retailers about the processes and demands of developing a joint programme from the perspective of a retailer, and to offer a testimonial of the benefits of working with the retail team at MMU.

The University Perspective on the Partnership

MMU had responded to the Leitch Report (2006) and research by the Retail Sector Skills Council (SSC) Skillsmart Retail (2007) by working in partnership with Foundation Degree Forward (**fdf**) to develop a work based learning Foundation Degree in Retailing for the sector. In so doing it recognised that developing higher education provision that meets the needs of employees within the retail sector requires an approach to both development and delivery of HE that is tailored to the needs of the sector and the employers within it. A key element of the development therefore recognised that the learning and teaching of such a programme needed to 'go to the employer and their learners', rather than the learners 'coming to the university'.

Early indications that the programme met the needs of employers and employees in the sector were provided by the decision of a number of retail organisations including Booths to enrol their managers and trainee managers on the programme. In the case of Booths, an initial independent assessment of their in-house (MDP) by the **fdf** EBTA project enabled MMU to consider admitting Booths managers onto the programme with advanced standing. This also demonstrated the 'fit' between the FD and the management development requirements of retail organisations.

A key element in the approach to development and delivery of HE tailored to the needs of employers referred to above is an ability to react within the timescales required by businesses. To this end, MMU was able to rapidly assess the Booths MDP using the EBTA initial signposting and apply APEL to all managers who had successfully completed the Booths in-house programme.

A logical 'next step' in the development of a partnership between MMU and Booths was to integrate the Booths MDP and the Foundation degree (FD). Further work by EBTA consultants enabled Booths to enhance its MDP to provide assessment activities and a project with the ambition of providing equivalence of 50% of the FD (equivalent to 120 credits). This required a formal 'Collaborative Partnership' usually developed between a university and a 'college' learning provider such as a further education college or a private sector equivalent. It was vital that the process for accomplishing this was tailored to the unique needs of a retail business/university partnership. In these circumstances, either the university's process would need to change, or appropriate flexibility would need to be shown by the university (and to an extent by the employer). The key to achieving the partnership in a flexible manner required individuals who themselves were flexible by virtue of their background and experience. In the case of MMU, the requirement was for academics who understood (retail) businesses, and their people development goals. In the case of Booths, the requirement was for a champion for the partnership who had insights into the workings of HE and its quality control requirements. Fortunately, such individuals were present in both organisations and were able to drive the partnership process. In general, for such partnerships to develop successfully there needs to be mutual understanding through use of common language together with a mutual awareness of expectations and anticipations with regard to pace and timescales.

The practical effect of the collaboration as far as MMU is concerned is that the on the job training provided as part of the Booths MDP will be recognised as forming half of the FD programme. MMU 'Link Tutors' will work with Booths trainers to provide advice and guidance on assessment and ensure that the quality controls MMU applies to its own programmes apply just as rigorously to the Booths element of the FD. There will be mutual benefit in staff development terms. Booths staff will clearly benefit from the academic experience of the MMU tutors involved in the programme. The benefit for MMU will be that the currency and practicality of the FD will be enhanced by the involvement of retail practitioners and MMU staff will develop the skills required to operate comfortably in the contemporary world of the UK retail employer. HE as provided by MMU will be accessible to potentially large numbers of learners in full-time employment so demonstrating 'widening participation' outside of the normal (unemployed full-time) student.

Lessons Learned

- The world of HE and the business world do not speak a common language and do not necessarily understand each other's business imperatives. It is therefore important that, at the beginning of a partnership between an employer and a university, the representatives of the respective organisations recognise this fact and work to develop a common language and flexible procedures

- It is important that the partners recognise each other's objectives, strategic goals and strengths. This will prevent misunderstandings associated with perception of poor/inadequate response and timescales. For example, businesses sometimes perceive universities as not reacting rapidly enough to their requirements

- Universities for their part have quality of learning as a key strategic goal and therefore have processes for quality assurance and enhancement. These processes, as operated for the usual student (i.e. an individual studying full-time at the university) and a standard three-year degree programme, require a particular time-period to complete

- A mutually agreeable timescale for a partnership activity is achievable if the business recognises the university's strategic requirement and its importance to the goals of the partnership and if the university is able to adapt those processes to meet the business's needs

- The experience of the Booths/MMU partnership is that providing representatives of the organisations who are able to understand the differing worlds (of the retail business and the higher education provider) and operate comfortably across them mitigates the culture clash that may occur as these two worlds interact

- It is important that the respective organisations are represented by people who are able to champion the partnership (and its objectives) and 'trouble –shoot' on its behalf within their respective organisations. To a great extent this was the key to the success of the Booths/MMU partnership.

References

Booths (2007) Guide to Management Development Programmes: an overview (unpublished)

MMU Business School, Foundation Degree in Retailing Student Handbook

CHAPTER 3

Cathedrals Leave No Stone Unturned

Frances Cambrook, Associate Director, **fdf**

Brigadier Peter Lyddon, Administrator, Cathedrals Workshop Fellowship

Executive Summary

The Cathedrals Workshops Fellowship (CWF) is a partnership of Anglican cathedrals that maintain in-house stone workshops and undertake the training and development of stonemason apprentices. The CWF has designed an in-house training programme to formalise and standardise the later stages of stonemasonry apprentices' training and gain recognition for the higher level skills acquired by their apprentices. Through **fdf**'s EBTA scheme the University of Gloucestershire was chosen by the CWF as their Higher Education delivery partner. This case study highlights:

- A semi-generic shell framework provides a flexible mechanism for accrediting employers' training, provided the 'standard' elements can be made relevant to the employer's context

- Employers want to have clear lines of communication and do not need or want to understand a university's structures and project activity

- Work Based Learning (WBL) accreditation partnerships have the potential to offer wider benefits to the employer in terms of the impact on the workplace delivery staff which can be harnessed as CPD

- Providers tend to determine viability in terms of numbers, whilst an employer may be seeking long term impact on small numbers

Introduction and Background

The CWF is a partnership of eight Anglican Cathedrals, Durham, York, Lincoln, Canterbury, Winchester, Salisbury, Gloucester and Worcester. These Cathedrals are the only ones who still maintain their own onsite stone workshops; most now employ outside contractors to carry out the specialised work of restoring, repairing and conserving the stone fabric of these historic buildings. These commercial enterprises often do not support the training of apprentices; it is only in onsite workshops, with a continuing programme of work, that comprehensive training can take place. There is increasing concern about the long term future of these workshops, and the need to maintain a consistent standard of specialist skills and workmanship to sustain the ongoing repair and maintenance of the important historic buildings. It became clear during the course of a meeting in 2006 that a Fellowship of Cathedral Workshops might be able to offer additional benefits, not only to participating Cathedrals, but also perhaps by helping with the long term maintenance of those Cathedrals without works departments, as well as the many thousands of churches and heritage sites throughout the country which are in a state of disrepair. It did not take long to establish a system of self-help and cooperation, to arrange exchange schemes between the workshops, and to agree that a four year stonemason apprenticeship should be the standard for all.

The CWF team developed a series of work based units of study which all Cathedral stone mason apprentices need to complete. The programme was designed to develop apprentices from entry at level 2 through to level 4/5 in the first instance. The individual Cathedrals already had working relationships with a number of universities and colleges, but the Fellowship wanted to establish a new collaborative partnership for the higher level training programme they had designed. The CWF contacted **fdf** in 2008 seeking specialist advice and support to gain accreditation of the new course. Through its EBTA service **fdf** helped the CWF to secure accreditation of their programme and the first cohort of Foundation Degree students enrolled with the University of Gloucestershire in January 2010.

Evaluation and Partner Selection

The course that the CWF had designed, without realising it, was an embryonic Foundation degree, with the key characteristics of the qualification already in place: work based learning, flexibility and employer involvement. All that was needed was a university partner with whom the CWF could work to achieve validation of the course, and the **fdf** EBTA service provided the mechanism and process for achieving that. Initial work was done to translate the input-oriented training the CWF had articulated into the outcomes-based approach of UK Higher Education. Once the outline modules were in a general style and form which could be recognised by a university, with indicative credit values and learning volume identified the process of selecting a university partner commenced. Expressions of interest were sought and a rigorous selection process took place. This was important to the CWF, to enable them to explore in depth the nature of the proposed relationship and to make an informed choice of partner. A key factor for the CWF was to feel confident that they would retain ownership of their course. The University of Gloucestershire was selected as the validation partner.

Validation

The University of Gloucestershire has a flexible 'shell' qualification framework designed specifically to make it easier to respond to and work with employers, so this made the validation exercise relatively straightforward. Figure 2.1 shows the overall structure of the shell framework. The process took approximately four months from the date of the first post-selection meeting, and was mainly carried out remotely. Throughout this time *fdf* maintained active involvement in the process, supporting the parallel development of Level 5 as well as advising and supporting the CWF as they began the process of putting the Level 4 programme into operation.

Figure 2.1: The University of Gloucestershire Shell Framework[1]

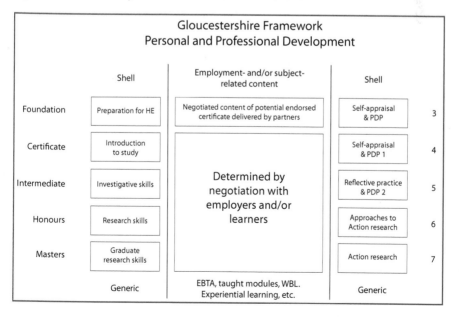

		Gloucestershire Framework Personal and Professional Development		
	Shell	Employment- and/or subject-related content	Shell	
Foundation	Preparation for HE	Negotiated content of potential endorsed certificate delivered by partners	Self-appraisal & PDP	3
Certificate	Introduction to study		Self-appraisal & PDP 1	4
Intermediate	Investigative skills	Determined by negotiation with employers and/or learners	Reflective practice & PDP 2	5
Honours	Research skills		Approaches to Action research	6
Masters	Graduate research skills		Action research	7
	Generic	EBTA, taught modules, WBL. Experiential learning, etc.	Generic	

The University confirmed the findings of the preliminary evaluation of the CWF units, and a Level 4 pilot year was implemented, whereby students worked towards a Foundation Degree in Personal and Professional Development (Stonemasonry). There was growing awareness of the practical implications for the CWF staff of actually delivering the programme, and a feeling that a staged development process might be wise. Figure 2.2 shows the configuration of the programme.

Figure 2.2: The CWF programme

Level 4	Shell Module						Shell Module
	Introduction to Study (Stone Types)	Structural Materials & Fixing	Archaeology of Historical Buildings 1	Architectural History & Styles 1	Stone Conservation	Setting Out	Self Appraisal and PDPI
Credits	15	15	15	20	20	20	15

Level 5	Shell Module					Shell Module
	Investigative Skills	Stone Conserv-ation 2	Historical Ornamental Carving	Architectural History and Archaeology	Work Based Project	Self-Appraisal and PDP II
Credits	15	15	15	30	30	15

At the time, the University had a HEFCE-funded Higher Skills project called Nexus, dedicated to working with local employers to develop work based courses, and the University decided that Nexus would be the most appropriate host for the programme This arrangement worked reasonably well in terms of practicalities, and offered access to premises and facilities for group sessions which proved extremely useful. However, it created a shift in terms of relationships at a critical stage in the development of the partnership between the CWF and the University, which at times the CWF struggled to understand. This highlights the importance of universities having clear and straightforward systems in place for communicating with employers and managing partnerships, ensuring that the 'wiring' is hidden (as much as possible).Nexus were also involved to enable access to funding to support the pilot phase. As an employer engagement project, it enabled a relatively low-cost model to be developed which recognised the in-kind contribution that the CWF were making through delivering the programme themselves. Nonetheless, there was a need for additional funding to make the programme operationally viable, and the CWF and University were successful in securing sponsorship from a major heritage-related company, the Ecclesiastical Insurance Group (EIG).

Delivery of Pilot Programme

The Level 4 programme commenced with a cohort of seven students from five of the participating cathedrals. The students were selected by the cathedrals according to the current stage of their training, their experience and their perceived suitability and capability to benefit from the programme. The programme was delivered as a series of three long weekend teaching blocks, which were all based at Nexus in Gloucester, with on-site work at Gloucester Cathedral and additional field trips. Students then returned to their Cathedrals and continued to apply the learning from the blocks both in their assignment preparation and their every day work, the two being integrated and aligned as much as possible. A final face to face assessment block took place at the end of the programme at which the practical elements were assessed on-site at Winchester Cathedral. This model of delivery was adopted in an effort to maximise the benefits of bringing the students together for face to face activity, whilst minimising the work and domestic disruption for both students and staff.

The venue and facilities at Nexus were excellent, and the geographical location relatively convenient for most participants. However, the lack of engagement with a variety of cathedral locations, and the access to a wider range of potential field trips this would have afforded, was identified as a shortcoming and as a result it was decided to deliver each of the teaching blocks for the Level 5 programme at different cathedrals. In addition, it was recognised that delivery at weekends was problematic for both students and staff, in terms of tiredness and travel, so delivery is now on weekdays.

Ongoing Support and Development

It was recognised by both the University and the CWF that there was a need for informed continuity in terms of liaison between the partners, and **fdf** involvement therefore continued throughout this period. The EBTA consultant fulfilled two roles – the quality assurance role normally undertaken by a university link tutor was effectively 'sub-contracted', and the employer continued to be supported in developing the processes and procedures for delivering their training. It is fair to say that the impact and implications for the CWF in actually delivering their programme had not been fully appreciated, and this raises interesting issues with regard to EBTA engagements in terms of establishing employers' capacity to deliver validated or accredited provision effectively, particularly where there may not be an existing training department, nor indeed any experience of coordinating training across an organisation. This type of activity has come to be known as 'EBTA plus' and has significant implications and potential in terms of widening participation in the EBTA service to businesses and organisations who might otherwise be unable to undertake HE accredited training.

Outcomes and Impact

Overall and to date, the pilot Level 4 and Level 5 years have been successful, if challenging. All the students indicated a broadly positive experience:

> 'this programme has given me the ability to communicate with confidence in what I am saying, to people whom I was initially intimidated by'.

> 'Not many courses allow you to learn on the job and put your skills straight into practice. Knowing that there is an official qualification there at the end of the course is an added motivation, it is good to know that our efforts will be officially recognised.'

The key generic issue emerging from analysis of student feedback and module reports was the need for better identification of, and access to, relevant resources to support learning. This highlights an interesting dilemma when developing niche provision, particularly in a practical subject area with a geographically dispersed cohort; exactly what resources are needed as a minimum, where should these be located and how can they be accessed? The need to accommodate the generic shell modules, particularly PDP, raised some challenges for the CWF team and indeed potentially raises wider issues with regard to the integration of institutionally-developed modules which are designed to operate without a specific context, where there is in fact a very specific context already in place.

In terms of the employer's perspective, all of the cathedrals with students on the pilot programme reported a positive impact on the participating individuals, the wider team and the training staff themselves. Students are seen to be more focused and committed to the development of their practical skills and more aware of the wider context in which they operate. They are reported to be more confident and better able to articulate and communicate their ideas. This has a knock-on effect within the stonemasonry and wider works teams, with active interest from other staff, both younger apprentices and more senior staff who do not have formal qualifications themselves, in participating in the programme in future.

An unintended, or at least unanticipated, consequence was on staff involved in the delivery and support of the students. Most had no recent or prior knowledge of the Higher Education system. The University has provided essential and well-received development sessions, particularly around assessment, and there are plans to develop accredited CPD modules for the staff so that they can also gain recognition for **their** work based learning. The commitment and time of the CWF Administrator, a volunteer, who has extensive knowledge and experience of the Cathedral working and training environment, has been a critical success factor, and the need for this role in establishing a sustainable programme has been noted. Staff have commented:

'We needed to act decisively as we faced the very real prospect that in 20 years time we would be left without sufficient skilled craftspeople. We knew we had a good quality in-house training provision but we needed the expertise that **fdf** provides to take us forward. The support provided through EBTA was invaluable, without it I'm not sure we would find ourselves in the positive position we do today'.

And in terms of the University, it has also learned important new lessons, as Professor Stephen Hill, Dean of Teaching and Learning Innovation explains:

'This project has been very important to the University as we would not necessarily have run this type of qualification on our own. It has given us an opportunity to work in partnership with both the CWF and **fdf** to develop something new and has become a valuable strategic exercise. Through our involvement with EBTA it has demonstrated all sorts of issues that the University needs to be able to tackle, but also it will prove that we can develop partnerships and projects that are sustainable in the long-term. It has given us a valuable insight into exactly what an employer-led curriculum means from a Higher Education perspective.'

Looking Ahead

It is probably fair to say that no-one involved, whether from the Fellowship, the University, **fdf** or the students themselves fully appreciated what they were taking on when they embarked on this journey. Clearly the initiative has benefited from, and capitalised on, a particular set of circumstances in the world of skills development which provided access to human and financial resources to pump prime the endeavour. Whilst this may call into question whether, or at least when, the project might have been realised without this support, it should not be taken as a negative indicator with regard to the potential for similar initiatives. The essential thinking has been done, and a model devised, which has significant potential for further and wider application and development, which the CWF is keen to take forward into the wider stonemasonry sector.

Clearly there are challenges: small numbers of geographically dispersed students, extremely busy staff needing to find time to deliver the programme and assess the learning. This inevitably raises the question as to whether the programme is sustainable, and indeed whether the investment has been worth making in the first place. The answer to both of these is yes, but for more important reasons than cohort size or cost. Cathedrals have business plans like any other business, but have works plans which operate over much longer periods – five, ten or even twenty years, with a corresponding need for long term investment in associated craft skills, no matter how small scale and specialist. The CWF has gone some way towards creating an efficient approach to training which has the potential to be expanded and extended in time, firstly and most immediately to the wider stonemasonry workforce, and secondly to embrace a broader range of specialist practitioners, thereby increasing viability if not profitability.

What the CWF has demonstrated is that it is possible to take the initiative and determine and influence the nature of training, and that it is possible to demonstrate that the development and application of craft skills can operate at a higher level.

However, the fundamental issue which challenges this and similar work based programmes developed under the auspices of EBTA, is the long term maintenance of the operational aspects of the partnership in such a way as to satisfy the twin demands of the employer for a straightforward method of working with an HEI and the HEI for confidence that a programme is being delivered in accordance with HE quality assurance procedures. The 'luxury' of publicly funded mediators, whether from **fdf** or one of the university-based employer engagement projects, will disappear as these initiatives and projects come to a natural end, and there is a need to address the implications of this for the sustainability and stability of many work based programmes. It may be that there is a need for a new role and financial model, which draws on the good practice developed through initiatives such as the CWF programme discussed here, one which defines the minimum requirement for provision based employer-provider partnerships and establishes the true cost for employers of actively engaging with Higher Education.

Lessons Learned

- Creating a completely new higher level programme with an employer with no prior experience of formally delivering higher level training or of the university sector, takes time, patience and persistence, but the results in terms of impact on all parties to the endeavour, employer, employee and provider can exceed expectations

- Viability and sustainability are not just about numbers; in this sector, better the right course for a few, for decades to come, than the wrong (or no) provision for many

- To be successful a WBL partnership requires a long term commitment beyond the accreditation exercise and employers and providers need to have the resources and drive to sustain this

- The positive developmental impact on the work based trainers was an unintended but welcome benefit

Endnotes

1   If interested, please contact Professor Stephen Hill, shill@glos.ac.uk)

CHAPTER 4

Practical Challenges of Accreditation: the Croda International New Manager Programme

Ann Minton, Workforce Development Fellow, University of Derby Corporate

and

Nigel Fenwick, Group Training Advisor, Croda International plc

Executive Summary

This case study discusses the practical challenges for the company and the University, associated with the accreditation of an established in company programme. We outline the background to the programme, and its foundation within the company vision, explaining how this was evaluated and translated into a recognisable HE programme. The key elements that have made this a successful partnership are discussed, outlining the key challenges that both the company and the University faced. The key learning points are the development of a partnership of equals, where each partner respects what the other brings to the development; the sharing of philosophy in the approach to teaching and learning strategy and finally, the need for clear and concise communication between organisations at all levels.

Background: Rationale and Development of the Programme

Croda International plc (Croda) is a world leader in the manufacture of natural based speciality chemicals sold to virtually every type of industry. Formed in 1925 they operate in 34 countries worldwide, with approximately 3400 employees. A FTSE 250 company, with year-on-year increases in operating profit, Croda has a clear vision for the company:

The Croda Vision

- To remain an independent company and operate as one global team
- We will remain a 'fun', lively, stimulating place of work, where all employees have the courage to question, and all functions and individuals are valued
- There will be a place for many styles of leadership, but all leaders will have as their primary objective to build other leaders
- We can only achieve our goals through excellent and constant communication, creativity and setting clear objectives at every level
- We will continually improve
- We will continue to be an ethical and responsible company

(Croda plc, 2007)

The New Manager programme was developed in 2007 to fulfil a gap in the development of new people managers within the company and aligns management development training to the Croda vision. It encourages the application of the learning, and therefore the vision, during the first six to twelve months of a new manager being in such a role.

There was recognition that many new managers had graduate level knowledge and skills in subjects related to their role (e.g. chemists, lawyers) or had developed significant experience within the company to conduct their role, but few had knowledge and skills related to leadership and management. Minzberg (2003: 1) recognises this issue:

'we need to build the craft and the art of managing into management education and thereby bring these back into the practice of managing'.

At the beginning of 2011, 65 managers, across the UK and Europe had successfully completed the programme, with a further 15 delegates starting the programme in January 2011.

The company recognised that the programme has had a clear beneficial impact on its management population, with managers demonstrating:

- An increase in confidence when approaching a people management related situation

- Increased awareness and application of techniques and styles, resulting in improvement of performance of the team

- Improvement in the clarity and definition of objectives and personal development plans for team members

- Improvement in the ability to prioritise the activities of the team

- A willingness and desire to network with other managers of the same level to share experiences and learn from each other

Croda felt that these benefits would be more tangible if they were recognised by an external organisation. Consequently, Croda approached the University of Derby to accredit the New Manager programme at HE level.

Programme Overview

The Croda programme contains eight, monthly, one day sessions. Each session has its own theme, but fits within the overarching theme of Managing People. This can broadly be divided into managing teams and motivating and developing individuals. The University programme therefore consists of two modules based upon these themes.

Defined post-session activities encourage the application of learning between sessions. These activities are then reflected on holistically at the end of the module in the context of managing the team or developing the individuals. The reflections articulate the impact that the learning has had on the team, the individuals and within the business. An end of programme presentation by delegates to the senior executives reflects on the impact of their own personal development.

Croda Sessions University Modules

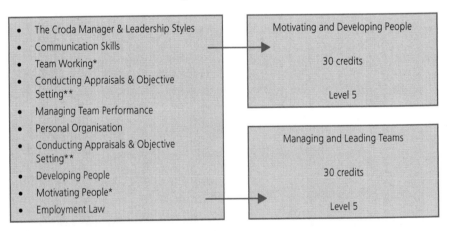

* Motivating People and Team Working is one session

** Conducting Appraisals and Objective Setting sessions applicable to both University modules.

Thus successful completion of the whole programme leads to a University Diploma in Managing People (60 credits at level 5)

Challenges Faced in the Accreditation Process by the University and the Company

The key challenge faced by both organisations was to find a way of articulating the alignment of the programme to Higher Education expectations whilst maintaining its focus on the business need and reflecting the business language.

Key Challenges for Croda Include:

- **Maintaining the integrity of the existing programme that has been proven to meet the business need**. The programme content was determined from consultation meetings between senior managers and the training team, and was deemed to be the essential developmental events needed for new managers. The content was also constructively aligned (Biggs, 1996) to the Croda vision, each session is structured to build on the learning from preceding sessions. The programme portrays a balance of what managing people actually involves, i.e. positive aspects such as developing people but also challenging ones such as dealing with conduct and capability issues. Croda recognises that the programme meets the business need and changes to the programme to meet the requirement of an external qualification framework would potentially compromise this.

- **Finding a partner that has synergies with the company approach**. A number of institutions were analysed by Croda to determine if a HE qualification could be mapped to the New Manager Programme. In most cases, Croda would have had to completely change the programme to meet their requirements. Only the University of Derby Corporate gave assurances that the current New Manager Programme framework could be maintained whilst providing the means of a HE qualification.

- **Understanding academic language and quality assurance mechanisms**. Although many Croda employees are graduates, academic language is not commonplace in their day-to-day vocabulary. This became very apparent in the joint production of the validation documents, which were written and structured to fit with the University's quality process, with some of the terminology being new and unfamiliar to Croda. Some of the Croda terminology clashed with that of the University. For example, Croda called each session a module, but the University's module was each 30 credit unit. Croda therefore adapted their terminology. Croda was not used to formal quality assurance mechanisms within its training and development department, using more informal methods such as course evaluations and post-course impact of learning to evaluate the provision. Thus being faced with lengthy quality assurance documentation, in academic jargon, was somewhat daunting. Croda appreciated that these university protocols were essential to the accreditation process and were fully supported throughout their production.

- **Balancing business timeframes and academic processes**. Croda was used to working very quickly when it came to translating a business proposal into reality and providing business benefits. There was an appreciation from both parties that timescales of working were culturally different, but adapting to each others' needs was crucial. Croda understood that the University had structures and quality assurance factors to adhere to and was therefore patient with its timescales. The University understood that a commercial business acts and reacts very quickly and was, therefore, determined to develop approval processes that were proportionate and fit for purpose for a 60 credit qualification at level 5.

Challenges from the University's perspective

- **Articulation of the mapping process of company provision to HE standards**. For approval of the Croda course the University must be satisfied that the learning is aligned to HE benchmarks and standards, this involves the review of the curriculum, its aims and expected outcomes, alongside the typical role profile and role descriptions of the potential delegates.

The University of Derby has found that the use of Level Indicators (e.g. SEEC, 2010 or Durrant, Rhodes and Young, 2009) provides an excellent mechanism for articulating the mapping, as they generically reflect the QAA's Framework for Higher Education Qualifications (FHEQ) and can be contextualised to the benchmark statements. The emphasis of the pedagogical approach and assessment strategy was clearly on the application of learning in the work place, using the workplace as the locus to inform and drive the learning process – the situated learning approach recognised by Lave and Wenger (1991). Articulation of the volume of credit represented used notional learning hours (1 credit equating to 10 notional hours of learning). Consideration being given to the period of time over which the learning took place (9 months) and the amount of time spent on applying the learning in the work place to determine an appropriate volume of credit.

- **Articulating the provision in language that both the company and HE recognise**. Whilst the programme has to be recognisable as HE to gain approval for academic credit it also needs to be recognisable within the company, reflecting the Croda vision, the business needs and the expectations of the company for its managers. Learning outcomes therefore had to be written that reflected the academic level, knowledge and skills, but also the company expectations of their managers. A single set of learning outcomes were developed that embraced both the academic and business requirements, so that both aspects of the programme were inextricably linked and of equal importance. The level indicators, reflecting academic level and founded in work based learning were easily contextualised to leadership and management learning outcomes.

- **Developing an appropriate Assessment Strategy.** The development team from the University and Croda reviewed the existing assessment activity identifying that the 'post module' work (undertaken by the delegates between sessions) and the final presentation could be used for assessment purposes, as they clearly demonstrated achievement of the learning outcomes. Furthermore the post module activities were founded in 'real work' activity, recognised by Boud and Solomon (2001) as being one of the key characteristics of work based learning. The use of the post module activities also facilitated an incremental approach to assessment. So that the learning could be applied in a systematic manner the team discussed the need to embed the academic writing skills within the assessment activity to ensure that referencing to theory and models was undertaken appropriately. This required brief additions to the guidance notes that accompanied the activity to emphasise the need for referencing. The team discussed the holistic review of the individual activities, to bring the learning together, reflect on impact and identify further development and learning needs and opportunities.

Support and guidance for assessment were largely in place, there were clear guidelines associated with the post module activities, with opportunities for formative feedback on the written work. Indeed this guidance was very helpful during the mapping phase to identify the academic level and content of the programme. A presentation with voice over was developed, by a University tutor, to support the production of the reflective summaries. This approach was adopted to emphasise the link with the University and to introduce new media for support purposes.

- **Developing proportionate University approval processes that are fit for purpose**. According to the QAA the partnership between the University and Croda falls within the definition of 'collaborative provision' in that it leads to an award of the University that is 'delivered and/or supported and/or assessed through an arrangement with a partner organisation.' (QAA, 2010). Thus, the approval mechanisms need to reflect the collaborative nature of the programme. However, it was important to recognise that there are significant differences between this provision and more traditional types of collaborative provision of delivery of major awards by Further Education colleges or overseas HE institutions. For this development it was therefore necessary to adopt a risk-proportionate approach to approval that reflected the academic level and credit tariff (60 credits at level 5). The approvals process had to be robust, but within a business timeframe. Documentation needed to reflect that this was a relatively small programme, which had been successfully delivered by the company for a number of years. A partner profile document providing an overview of the company (and the training department particularly) together with the resources available to support delegate learning was prepared. An operational manual documented the programme management arrangements between the University and Croda, so that there was clarity of expectation and responsibility for both organisations.

External advice was sought to confirm that:

- the mapping of the Croda programme to HE standards had been appropriately conducted

- the teaching, learning and assessment strategy was appropriate for the subject, level and volume of credit awarded

- the arrangements for delegate support and guidance were clearly articulated and appropriate to HE

- the quality assurance and management arrangements were appropriate and fit for purpose

Ongoing Quality Assurance

There is close liaison between the University and Croda team to design and implement the induction programme, develop assessment guidance for delegates and to write formative feedback. First marking of the written work and presentations is undertaken by the Croda team, with second, independent, marking undertaken by the University team. When marks and comments have been compared there is complete agreement on the mark awarded and broad agreement of comments for summative feedback to the delegates. Given the level of consistency of marks and feedback, a sample of work will now be moderated by the University. If there is a change in personnel, assessment method, or a recommendation from the internal or external moderator about the quality and standards of marking, second marking will be reintroduced.

External moderation is undertaken, according to usual University practice and considered by an assessment board. The external examiner confirms to the board that the quality and standards on the Croda programme are the same as for other HE programmes.

An annual report is produced that reflects on all aspects of the programme: the curriculum design, teaching and learning strategy, assessment method, delegate support and guidance, delegate achievement and programme management arrangements. The report draws on the reflections of the tutorial team from Croda and the University, the report of external moderator and delegate feedback. Staff development activities and requirements are also identified within the report and an enhancement plan produced for the forthcoming cycle. The report is then considered within the faculty quality processes and deliberative structures and by the HR manager at Croda.

The University recognised that many of its employer partner tutors were very experienced trainers and adult educators, but had limited experience of HE processes. A 30 credit Certificate of Achievement 'Supporting Work Based learning in Higher Education' has therefore been developed by the University to recognise the needs of this diverse range of learners and also to create an emerging community of practice in this area.

Benefits

There are a number of benefits to Croda. Firstly, it has an internal development programme that has become externally accredited. This gives the New Manager Programme a higher level of value within the business and provides evidence that the Training and Development function is providing a programme of high quality and recognition. Secondly, Croda has taken the first step in developing what is hoped will be a long-term partnership with the University of Derby Corporate. There is opportunity to scope other internal development programmes that Croda currently has in its training and development portfolio, giving a wider range of Croda employees the opportunity to gain HE qualifications.

A key benefit to the individual is the added value that an external university / HE qualification brings. The New Manager Programme was already internally certified but feedback from delegates reveals that having a university certification brings added satisfaction and will also enhance their CV, as they have gained a university-based qualification that recognises their HE level achievement in people management.

Summary: Key Learning Points

The success of the accreditation partnership between the University and Croda is founded in a shared goal and philosophy of learning: the application of theory to benefit the business. The pedagogical approach to teaching learning and assessing was based on the underpinning work based learning philosophy of both organisations and reflects Boud and Solomon's (2001) characteristics of work based learning.

The development was founded on the principle of true and equal partnership, with the University offering a framework of quality assurance within which the Croda programme could be delivered. Both organisations have recognised the expertise within the other and have valued the expertise and learned from each other. The University has listened closely to the Croda experience of the quality assurance processes and has reflected again on the nature of the provision and the need to meet business timescales. Croda has drawn on the expertise of the University in technology enhanced learning and assessments to enhance support for delegates who are distant form the training team.

This development and willingness to share can only be conducted where there is trust at all levels of the partnership, with good communication channels between tutorial and operational teams, and a willingness to listen to each other's perspective to enhance the University process and the delegate learning experience.

References:

Biggs J (1996) 'Enhancing teaching through constructive alignment.' *Higher Education*. Volume 32 / Number 3: pp. 347–364,

Boud D and Solomon N (2001) *Work-Based Learning: A New Higher Education?* (Milton Keynes: Society for Research into Higher Education & Open University Press)

Croda plc (2007) The Croda Vision unpublished

Durrant A., Rhodes G. and Young D. (eds) (2009) *Getting Started with University Level Work Based Learning*. (Faringdon; Libri publishing) pp. 87–91

Lave J. and Wenger E. (1991) *Situated Learning: Legitimate Peripheral Participation* (Cambridge: Cambridge University Press)

Minzberg H (2004) *Managers, Not MBAs: A Hard Look At The Soft Practice Of Managing And Management Development*. (San Francisco: Berrett –Koehler)

SEEC (2010) Credit level descriptors for Higher Education. Southern England Consortium for Credit Accumulation and Transfer.

available at http://www.seec.org.uk/publications/seec-credit-level-descriptors-2010-revised-2004 (accessed 29/3/2011)

QAA (2010) Code Of Practice For The Assurance Of Academic Quality And Standards In Higher Education.

Section 2: Collaborative provision and flexible and distributed learning (including e-learning) – Amplified version October 2010

Available at http://www.qaa.ac.uk/academicinfrastructure/codeOfPractice/section2/collab2010.pdf (accessed 29/3/2011)

CHAPTER 5

A Sparkling Example of Employer-University Engagement: Measuring Programme Impact

Dr Paul Spear, Academic and Business Development Manager, The Leading Edge, University of Leicester, Former De Beers (Accreditation) Project Manager

Christopher (Kip) Jeffrey*, Senior Lecturer in Industrial Rocks and Minerals, Course Director De Beers Diamond Professional Programme, University of Leicester

Angela O'Brien, Accreditation Programme Manager, De Beers UK Ltd

Executive Summary

De Beers required a university able to develop a bespoke talent development programme with a specialist diamond industry curriculum encompassing diamond geology and science, practical diamond sorting and gemmology, sales, marketing, retail and industry issues. The rigorous tender process resulted in the University of Leicester being awarded the contract with the development of the Diamond Professional Programme, a sixty credit, level 6 graduate certificate delivered through a creative blended learning model.

The University was able to instigate an impact and Return on Investment (ROI) study for the benefit of both parties. The ROI study has enabled De Beers to differentiate the first cohort of successful students and manage their expectations for future roles and promotions in the UK and southern Africa. The ROI illustrations have provided a

---

* Would readers please contact this person to discuss IPR issues if you are considering using any of the content of this chapter in your own organisation.

sense of scale to the programme and the steps and time scales required to realise a financial return. The immediate intangible benefits identified by the programme have been articulated at board level with De Beers continuing its partnership with the University of Leicester.

The Diamond Professional Programme is an exemplar of the following guiding principles of employer-university engagement:

- The leading players must take ownership of the project, defend it within their organisations and be sensitive to managing expectations provided the programme remains within the strategic plan of the employer

- The leading players in both organisations must have good communication skills and ideally be experienced project managers

- The project should be bound by a contract with unambiguous documentation regarding the scope, deliverables, budgets and payment schedules

- The employer lead should have a good appreciation of the HE sector and the administrative and approval processes of a university with particular understanding of Accreditation of Prior Learning (APL) and Accreditation of Prior Experiential Learning (APEL) processes

- For a high visibility programme, instigate the ROI study at the start of the course delivery, using it as a management tool, rather than retrospectively, and identify clear business metrics that the learners will focus on during and after the programme which have a chain of impact from the learning outcomes

Employer-university Engagement Strategy

As the world's leading rough diamond mining company, De Beers Group owns mines in southern Africa and Canada. The group has offices in the UK, Botswana, South Africa and Namibia. Annually, several billion dollars of rough gem diamonds are sorted into about 12,000 categories for valuation. The diamonds then undergo aggregation, a process of blending like-for-like categories irrespective of their country of origin, followed by splitting into types and quantities according to the requirements of the group's clients. There are ten sales weeks annually, known as Sights, held at Diamond Trading Company (DTC) offices, where the clients (the Sightholders) view the rough diamonds they have been offered for sale. Sightholders represent world-class diamond businesses across all of the world's trading centres, from dealers to jewellery manufacturers and retailers, and contribute to a global diamond jewellery market worth tens of billions of dollars annually.

Employees are fundamental to shaping the future of the De Beers Group. In 2006 De Beers, through its UK office, identified a need to raise and broaden its technical leadership and talent base across the global operations. At a high level the desired outcome was to develop a talent pool with a depth of diamond product and industry knowledge able to contextualise their roles, identify business issues and contribute to meeting strategic challenges. For individuals, needs included empowerment, enhanced technical and business decision making, perceiving their performance in terms of an enterprise view congruent with enhanced performance and taking on new roles. Organisational aims included an internally grown talent pool and improvements in collaborative working and organisational effectiveness.

The lead author was appointed as project manager to produce a concept and feasibility study for the development of an accredited higher education (HE) programme. The lead author had over 20 years experience with De Beers as a research physicist (publishing and patenting), educator, media communicator and international speaker on consumer confidence in diamonds and as a business analyst.

A number of options for the academic level were considered from level 5 to 7. Assessments of the HE sectors in southern Africa and the UK, followed by a rigorous tender process resulted in the University of Leicester being awarded a contract as the HE partner in 2007 with administration through its Department of Geology. The proposed Diamond Professional Programme (DPP) would be a level 6 Graduate Certificate award carrying sixty credits. The choice of a graduate level was to be important in relation to the admission process and also set a corporate benchmark and a respected 'signature' qualification.

The fundamental challenges ahead of the programme creators were the development of broad cross-discipline content and an optimal pedagogy and delivery and assessment process across the global DTC offices that would fit with the operational calendar and needs of the company. As important was the requirement for a rigorous meritocratic admission process based on formal qualifications, APL and APEL.

Programme Development Process

The development of the DPP and enrolment of the first cohort were managed strictly under PRINCE 2 methodology reporting into the De Beers UK board. The programme was fully funded by De Beers and had the approval of the Group Managing Director. There was senior management representation from across the DTC offices. The aim of project initiation was to instigate the university programme approval process and sign-off the university's business case, using full economic costing, against De Beers' development and programme delivery budgets. Full programme approval was achieved prior to the first cohort enrolment in September 2008. The breadth and depth of the programme development required engagement with the University of Leicester's Department of Geology in addition to significant input from industry specialists in De Beers and diamond jewellery marketing consultants.

The DPP comprises six modules that cut across the key disciplines within the diamond value chain: the value-adding business processes that transport and transform a rough diamond from the mine to a polished gem in the retail diamond jewellery market and that also maintains consumer confidence in the value of diamonds. Learners would not become specialists in the disciplines covered by the programme but become high level generalists able to understand, discuss and challenge with confidence the advice of specialists when leading or contributing to strategic projects.

The first five modules deliver diamond knowledge through the University of Leicester's Blackboard virtual learning environment (VLE) and develop gemmological skills (the technical and practical skills required to describe and identify the characteristics of coloured gemstones and gem diamonds) and practical rough diamond sorting skills at the DTC Diamond Academies (where the professional DTC diamond sorters are developed at the DTC offices). There are formative (non-examined) assessments to ensure students are progressing. The sixth module focuses on themes core to the diamond industry, such as promotion of business ethics, diamond nationalism, sustainability and consumer confidence. This final module especially requires the students to develop skills in critical analysis and industry insight.

The summative (examined) assessments, carried out in accordance with the University of Leicester's regulations, are made at each of four residentials held at the southern African DTC offices. Each lasting around a week, the residentials occur after modules 1, 3, 5 and 6. Diamond Academy instructors were given Associate University Tutor status in order to deliver practical content and a senior DTC diamond instructor was given Moderator status for the purposes of the practical examinations to ensure consistency of the assessment process. The following is a high level overview of the programme:

- **Module 1:** *Diamonds – Sources to Resources*
  Geology, Exploration, Mineral Resourcing and Mining Economics

- **Module 2:** *Gemmology and Diamond Science*
  Gemmology, Natural Diamonds, Synthetic Gem Diamonds, Diamond Simulants, Diamond Colour and Quality Treatments and their Detection and Disclosure

- **Module 3:** *Diamond Sorting and Valuation*
  Diamond Sorting, Valuation, Sales and Distribution Models, Rough and
  Polished Diamond Markets

- **Module 4:** *Diamond Sales and Marketing*
  Philosophy and Practice of Diamond Luxury Marketing, Branding, Consumer
  Demand and Retail

- **Module 5:** *International Diamond Business*
  Sustainable Development, Diamond Beneficiation (socio-economic benefits
  of diamond resources for diamond nations), International Kimberley Process,
  Operational Financial Review Analysis

- **Modules 6:** *Contemporary issues and complexity in the diamond industry*
  Discuss and critique cross cutting themes from Modules 1–5

- **Residential seminars:**
  Involving field trips to a diamond mine, cutting factories, luxury retailers and a
  De Beers industrial synthetic diamond manufacturing facility

- **Case study:**
  This threads and drives the overall programme, serving to integrate the
  knowledge and skills and acts as a significant vehicle for summative
  assessment

By September 2008 the DPP had enrolled its pilot cohort of nineteen students from
across the partner DTC offices. The pilot cohort was identified using a two-stage
process: De Beers' talent selection followed by a rigorous university process. The
university process involved the assigning of points to each candidate based on his/
her academic record, highest academic qualification, professional qualifications, APL
and APEL (reflecting a range of qualifications and backgrounds), and additionally the
competencies within their job grade compared to the HEFCE graduate skill set. This
was the essential contribution towards gaining programme approval. An accrued 10
points or over on the admission scoring secured a place on the programme subject
to sufficient budget.

The pilot cohort completed in August 2009 which was viewed by De Beers and
the University of Leicester as a success: all of the completing 16 students having
passed the programme. A second international cohort started in September 2010 for
completion in August 2011 and planning for a third cohort is underway.

Just prior to leaving De Beers in 2009, the lead author had wished to
accelerate the development of a process to measure and assess the impact and
value of the DPP to the learners, De Beers and the University of Leicester. The

Enterprise and Business Development Office at the University of Leicester secured an 'Innovations Partnership' grant through the HEFCE Economic Challenge Investment Fund for the lead author to continue to develop an impact study and capture and report the methodology in collaboration with the second author.

Measuring Outcomes and Impact

The principle purpose of evaluating the DPP is to ensure that the programme content, delivery and learning outcomes meet the needs of De Beers. The assessment of the impact of learning interventions is well established in the commercial sector. Phillips and Phillips (2008) have extended this approach to include the calculation of the monetary benefits (ROI) of a training or development programme. The Phillips methodology emphasises the necessity to demonstrate a chain of impact between the levels of evaluation, thorough planning of data recording and evaluation, use full costs and derive conservative financial benefits using trend analyses, control groups or expert estimates. In addition, the method promotes the contextual value of learning programmes through the intangible benefits. Briefly, the levels of reporting are (Phillips and Phillips, 2008):

- Level 1: Assessment of participant engagement
- Level 2: Assessment of learning
- Level 3: Assessment of the application of learning in the work place
- Level 4: Assessment of the business impact
- Level 5: Calculation of the Return on Investment (Net Benefits / Full costs), and the reporting of intangible benefits

The learners were requested to complete detailed questionnaires at the residentials which formed the basis of the data collection plan:

- At the final residential the students completed a detailed Business Impact Study questionnaire aligned to levels 1–4 in the Phillips methodology
- At the final residential Leicester issued an Overall Course Feedback questionnaire requiring the students to provide detailed contextual written feedback on the programme
- At each residential Leicester issued a Residential Questionnaire to assess the quality of teaching and the facilities

We therefore had a rich body of evidence on the quality of the pilot programme and qualitative measures of the students' intention to apply their learning and its impact. We have interrogated the data supplied by the pilot participants and the summative assessments at Level 2. This highlighted areas where improvements could be made in De Beers' and the University's processes to enhance the experience for the following cohorts.

In particular, assessment at Level 2 of the Phillips ROI methodology included plotting the learners' DPP admission scores against their final marks on the DPP. This plot indicated a linear correlation for each of two distinct populations of learners. The *Exceed* population achieved a higher level of marks compared to the *Achieve* population which is suggested as being a measure of the students' contextual value-added. Furthermore, it has been possible to identify participants with particular talents for strategic and critical thinking.

The questionnaires also asked the participants for their intentions and desire to apply the new knowledge and behaviours and their likely impact on the company providing qualitative Level 3 and Level 4 forecast data. These observations have allowed us to provide a management tool for De Beers, a performance and progression ladder, to assist in the selection of DPP 'graduates' for potential opportunities within their current role, create or contribute to departmental strategic projects and contribute to local operations groups or a global operational leadership group. The intention is to drive ROI through the creation of opportunities in the organisation.

At present De Beers is not in a position to quantify the full impact or ROI of the DPP. The calculation of an ROI estimate is sensitive to how we account for the development costs, whether we load against the pilot cohort or we prorate (apportion) across a number of cohorts on top of their respective delivery costs. In addition, we need to consider the time frame over which we track impact data and benefits. Talent development programmes contribute to the professional and personal growth of individuals, the results of which manifest over several years. It is therefore entirely appropriate that a one year development course such as the DPP should be monitored for at least three years after completion.

We have assisted this process by providing an ROI illustration. We have estimated net benefits over a period of three years for each of three cohorts following completion of the DPP. We use two proxy metrics:

(i) a conservative increase in performance (learners continue with what they did before the programme, but better, by for example improved decision making, cost efficiencies and shortened times to meet key performance indicators) of 10% valued at full salary costs by grade

(ii) The value of freeing up and transferring in the region of 5% of senior managers' time to those learners that were in the *Exceed* group only, for use in high level strategy work

Both these proxy metrics do not in themselves value the products or services that may be produced as outcomes of the use of the time, but use the fully loaded salaries to attempt an estimate of the base marginal value of extra contribution to the company. In the absence of data, the ROI illustration provides, importantly, a sense of the magnitude of the programme compared to its future benefits and the level of follow up required with the students.

The ROI illustration produced a modest positive ROI after two similar sized cohorts have completed the programme and contributed for at least three years. We believe prorating development costs over three cohorts and accruing benefits over three years is a robust and conservative approach. This highlights the long term nature of talent development programmes.

On returning to the company, all the learners 'graduating' from the first DPP were ready to contribute operationally or strategically to the business, empowered by their new knowledge and confidence. This was evidenced in the answers to the detailed questionnaires supplied as part of the data collection plan, personal meetings with their line managers and senior leadership teams. The learners' roles in the De Beers group of companies are quite diverse. The companies are tasked to develop meaningful business metrics for the learners following promotions or involvement in new opportunities.

The authors believe that the intangible benefits from the DPP can make a difference to the talent development strategy for De Beers. In terms of the individuals this includes personal empowerment, improved decision making and communication skills, a new enterprise view and wider opportunities. At the level of the organisation intangibles include an internally grown talent pool, improvements in collaborative working and organisational effectiveness. Indeed, the core intangible that formed the bedrock of the DPP was the need to embed knowledge and skills, hitherto the preserve of company specialists, within a generalist talent pool, that could be exploited in current or future management roles in order to demonstrate an awareness and contextualisation of the diamond business.

Lessons Learned

- A bespoke programme carries particular risks; the project scope, deliverables, timeline and budgets need to be clearly identified and agreed between parties, preferably through a contract

- It is vital to prevent project creep and ensure the employer's calendar is flexible enough to meet the more rigid academic calendar

- The leading players in each organisation must work and communicate well together. Having a lead academic at the university with core expertise and practical experience of the subject area(s) that complement the knowledge and experience of the employer lead is a real advantage

- Being able to set the appropriate 'university level' for the programme is crucial in helping to build a programme identity for the employer and manage the expectations of the prospective learners who must satisfy both the employer screening and university admissions procedures

- Conducting an impact and ROI study for a high visibility programme should ideally be built-in from the start, identifying key business metrics linked to the outcomes of the learning, and used as a management tool to drive the benefits throughout the delivery phase and when the learners return to the company

References

Philips P. P. and Phillips J. J. (editors) (2008), *Measurement and Evaluation Series*, John Wiley & Sons, Inc.

CHAPTER 6

A Journey in Practice: Upskilling the Workforce through Higher Education

Colin Kemp, Network Director, Halifax Bank

Tracey White, Senior Lecturer in Accreditation and Work Based Learning, Programme Leader HE Cert. Management Practice, Middlesex University

Introduction

Following uncertain times in the banking sector Halifax were clear about the need to restore customer confidence in banking. One of their key aims was to provide a consistently high standard of customer service in order to become Britain's 'best bank for customers'. This chapter will discuss how the Halifax's strategic plan to have the UK's best qualified staff in the sector has resulted in an accreditation of their in-house Operating Model, 'Journey in Practice' with progression onto a tailored award in Retail Banking Practice in partnership with Middlesex University. It will consider some aspects of the partnership approach to the employer engagement, programme design, development and implementation, the lessons learnt and the overall impact.

Background

The financial crisis in September 2008 left confidence in banking at rock bottom, not just for the public and for customers, but also for the thousands of front line workers in banks up and down the land. The humblest cashiers were indiscriminately labelled as 'bankers' and 'owned' by the tax-payer. The UK banking landscape had changed, and needed to change, forever. For the survivors, trust with customers had been shattered and needed to be re-built from the very foundations upwards. At the height of the crisis Halifax Bank of Scotland (HBOS) was acquired by Lloyds TSB to create Lloyds Banking Group. The Halifax brand and branch operations were retained, but it was recognised that if Halifax was to regain the trust of its customers, it would need to evidence that it had the most well-developed management team on the High Street.

Strategy

From this strategic imperative the company's 'Journey In Practice' (JiP) initiative was created. There were a number of core objectives the organisation was trying to achieve:

- Deliver a more consistent customer experience in each of the 670 Halifax branches

- Move from a 'sales' focus based on products, to a 'relationship' approach based on customers' needs

- Reduce bandwidth and achieve an uplift in overall performance, based on raising all branches to a higher, aggregate, standard of delivery

- Aspire to have the most qualified workforce on the high street

- Be able to objectively evidence that these standards and aspirations were being achieved

JiP created a single framework of activities ('solutions') that had been observed in the very best, high performing branches throughout the network and then created a process to embed them into every branch, every day. The operational challenge was all about getting 'buy-in' from (already busy) branch managers to implement something in a thoroughly consistent fashion, whilst at the same time encouraging them to stamp their own personalities all over it. Secondly, some previous 'change' programmes had not landed comprehensively, and there was a clear need to have a mechanism to make sure that JiP did, and that it could be evidenced.

Changing the working day routines in every branch and putting in a much more structured approach represented a very significant cultural change for the Halifax managers. The high street branches had clearly been very successful prior to this initiative, so creating the motivation to change working practices was going to be vital to realise the business benefits that had been identified.

It was recognised very early in the process by the Network Director from his previous experiences, that accreditation would be a vital component if the business was to truly evidence the changes externally, and to deeply embed the learning that was required. It was also a clear goal to offer the management teams the chance to obtain valuable, externally recognised, professional qualifications as part of the programme. For many, this proved to be the single biggest motivator in implementing JiP in a high quality way. This external accreditation created a tangible sense of pride in the achievement for individuals, and a sense of true investment by the company in them, and the brand. Indeed, accreditation in itself became a key internal differentiator.

JiP Accreditation

JiP is Halifax's internal operating model and a part of the process was going through an accreditation process with Middlesex University to develop a Halifax Certificate in Retail Banking Practice. It consists of three stages; Stage One is concerned with implementing the framework of solutions and Stage Two in embedding the solutions. The third stage progresses on to a University award where delegates consider the learning so far in the light of their local competitive environment and demonstrates the true value of the programme because it is voluntary, whereas stages One and Two are mandatory for all managers. Having mandatory elements proved to be valuable learning for the organisation because it got the programme mobilised and illustrated the total commitment of the Halifax to this process. There are two versions, one for Branch Managers which is equivalent to 30 credits at level 6, and one for the Local (area) Managers worth 40 credits at level 7. The accredited work is evidenced through a portfolio and consists of a range of activities and observations, which are supported by reflective learning statements, a SWOT analysis and action planning. Internally, successful completion of stages One and Two for these two workforces provides evidence of 'competence' and constitutes an employee's 'Licence to Operate'.

Process: a Partnership Approach

Halifax searched the market for a 'provider' and Middlesex University were identified as having both the expertise, and organisational commitment to be potential partners along with an impressive list of existing Work Based Learning relationships. A significant factor of Middlesex University that proved attractive to the company is that it recognises that expertise exists in organisational workplaces and that Universities are not the sole owners of knowledge, expertise and skills. However, both organisations had specific standards and expectations to be negotiated before engagement could be achieved. Halifax were clear that they did not want an examinations based approach and they required a very bespoke programme focused entirely on the JiP initiative, with 'credits' that were transferrable to higher qualifications if individuals wanted to take the learning on further.

Middlesex University, in turn, had exacting academic standards and learning style requirements if they were to put their name to the programme, and accrediting such a large scale change programme was new ground for the University. A true partnership approach was critical in taking this new initiative forward with each partner needing to understand the others context, work ethic, terminology etc. In particular, there was a range of people from Halifax involved in different stages of the programme, so Middlesex University had an important role to play in understanding the whole programme, its foundations, requirements and vision moving forwards in order to work with each new team as it became involved. Middlesex University grew to understand Halifax working practices and the timescales involved in delivering business in a changing landscape, which was quite a different culture from academia and the Middlesex University way. Meantime, it took a while for the Halifax team to understand fully that it was the learning, rather the Journey in Practice programme itself, which Middlesex University was accrediting. In the event both settled, after some significant negotiations, on the resultant programme. It has been important throughout the journey for both partners to listen to and understand each others requirements and to discuss this with the wider teams in both organizations and explore any potential problems or issues. With such a project and working with two large organisations, the team working ethic has been the foundation of the partnership approach. The Accreditation scheme is now a cornerstone of the Halifax JiP operating model and a huge success, with over a third of all Branch Managers registered for the voluntary University Award stage in the first full year of the programme, which is well ahead of projected take up. A significant factor of this success is that both the Halifax and Middlesex University are strongly committed to this partnership, which has given rise to a sense of shared ownership of the programmes and whose partnership approach is built upon mutual understanding and common rules of engagement.

Initially Middlesex University worked with consultants and representatives from Halifax to accredit the JiP programme. Halifax employed 32 JiP managers, (mostly from their branch manager ranks), to help embed the actual processes into their branches nationally, and these people became part of the first cohort to work with Middlesex University. Moving forwards a key element was to support these JiP managers, who were the internal coaches and became accredited assessors for the programme, with help to provide an understanding of the academic requirements, and in particular how they could enable colleagues to develop the appropriate reflective writing skills.

Progression

As JiP was being implemented throughout the organisation, negotiations and developments took place to provide a progression route for interested colleagues, known as Stage Three. This consisted of intense developmental activity between the two partners to develop bespoke negotiated work based projects and associated resources which built upon the accreditation and linked into business activity. This resulted in two programmes; an Advanced Diploma and a Post Graduate Certificate in Retail Banking Practice. The opportunity for branch managers to continue their learning with help from Halifax and Middlesex University beyond the mandatory stages was a very attractive part of the programme for individuals but in terms of creating engagement and 'buy-in' for the programme, the mandatory element of the accreditation was a defining factor of the success of the programme.

Outcomes

The Journey in Practice initiative was launched in to Halifax branches on January 1st 2010 with the first portfolios going to Middlesex University for review in March 2010. By the end of July, over 80% of Halifax branch managers had passed the first stage of JiP and received a Stage One Halifax Certificate in Retail Banking Practice.

By the end of 2010 over 50% of Halifax branch managers had passed Stage two, achieving 30 University credits and by the end of January 2011 a further 35 managers had completed the voluntary Stage three progression successfully achieving their Advanced Diploma in Retail Banking Practice At the time of writing (May 2011) over one third of eligible managers have already begun, or completed, Stage Three studies, with many more to follow as they graduate from Stage Two.

University learning has presented many challenges, opportunities and successes both for the Halifax as a whole and for individual learners. The traditional styles of learning within Halifax are significantly different from those being embraced within this programme and in particular the reflective learning approach was new and unfamiliar. Initially this was a challenge as the organisation as a whole needed to establish what was being expected, and develop a feel for reflective learning and writing.

This involved lots of support from the University and hard work in generating supporting materials which described these activities in familiar business language. Initially learners struggled to reach the necessary standard of reflective writing, but as they got to grips with the requirements, those same learners are now producing high quality work. A great success has been the realisation by many of the learners of the great value of reflection in improving performance. Halifax is a very fast paced organisation and typically colleagues struggle to build in time to reflect, often not seeing its value. This programme has opened many learners' eyes to the benefit of reflection in their work.

The JiP programme was a significant investment in building skills and behaviours to deliver tangible business and customer benefits. The financial business case created to secure the original investment from Lloyds Banking Group was clear about what was to be delivered, and by when. At the end of the first year, JiP was ahead of the target on benefits realisation on every measure. Customer service standards were improving, sales were above target levels and Colleague Satisfaction Survey results have continued to rise quarter on quarter at a time of unprecedented change. The Accreditation process has been at the heart of this success. The Reflective Learning Statements which sit at the core of the learning process have transformed the thinking styles of Halifax colleagues and their pride in having achieved recognised and valuable qualifications has been tangible.

As with any significant cultural change programme, there have been challenges. The intense nature of the accreditation process exposed some underlying weaknesses in some colleagues. Firstly, many were simply inexperienced in studying, and the concept of 'reflective' learning was alien and very difficult. The workload was, at times, onerous and maintaining standards was a considerable challenge, as was balancing study with the 'day job'. Halifax invested heavily in 32 dedicated coaches nationally to help colleagues with this work, and to ensure that the learning was being embedded, and evidenced through observations. At times, getting over 2,500 people through the various stages of accreditation at the pace needed proved challenging. The mandatory nature of the accreditation was a signal of real intent by the business, but in itself created some resistance at times. However, as colleagues emerged from Stage One successfully, along with the highly visible sharing of their success and reinforcement through tailored e-zine publications etc, the momentum gathered strongly to achieve the single most successful change programme Halifax has delivered in recent years.

The Halifax strategy was straight-forward: rebuild trust in its brand and help Lloyds Banking Group become the 'Best Bank for Customers'. To do that Halifax needed people who knew exactly what to do, how to do it and who got real motivation in the process. External accreditation of the Journey in Practice programme created that. The Middlesex University approach to reflective learning, evidence gathering (and tutoring) gave Halifax the opportunity to both realise and evidence the return from its investment.

CHAPTER 7

Facilitating Faster Growth with Small Enterprise

Tony Wall*, Senior Lecturer and Principal Investigator, Centre for Work Related Studies, University of Chester

Danielle Grant, Director, Leader*Shape*, Oxon UK

Executive Summary

Leader*Shape* is a group of business leaders who develop their clients' leadership capability, enabling the creation of high performance cultures through the coaching, mentoring and facilitation of individuals, peer groups and teams. It draws on their years of expertise in neuroscience, emotional intelligence and transpersonal leadership to enable change and growth for their clients. Contributing to a major growth initiative in the South of England, Leader*Shape* collaborated with the University of Chester to deliver a Postgraduate Certificate in Coach-Mentoring and Facilitation in Organisations for coaches of fast growing businesses. Subsequently, provision has expanded rapidly to include shorter accredited professional development courses and longer flexible awards to serve the complex development needs of today's organisational leaders, against a backdrop of increasing speed of change in line with Leader*Shape*'s developing intellectual property.

This case study highlights the following:

- Benefits of starting with a specific and manageable product with a clearly defined remit – then growing provision to meet developing opportunities

- Need to work closely, openly and regularly to meet the needs of, and to appropriately challenge, well-qualified, highly experienced professionals

---

*   Would readers please contact this person to discuss IPR issues if you are considering using any of the content of this chapter in your own organisation

- Importance of the alignment of required training outcomes and a shared commitment to the outcomes required for university level accreditation

- Importance and benefits of listening to participants to refine and develop practices and being flexible enough to adjust swiftly

- Benefits of a flexible, negotiated work based learning framework to enable the university to work flexibly with a training provider and to enable the training provider to react to and create new opportunities.

Facilitating Entrepreneurial Growth

LeaderShape has an excellent track record in the UK for facilitating high impact mentoring and coaching for example, the Merlin Mentoring programme, a three-year project to build a community of high-calibre mentors across the South East region. Having such an impressive track record in leadership development, LeaderShape secured their place as the key contributor to a £5 million European and Regional Development Fund project, 'Coaching for High Growth'. Led by Oxford Innovation, the UK's leading operator of Innovation Centres, the project is aimed at boosting the leadership performance in fast growing businesses in Cornwall through executive mentoring and coaching. Dr Treve Willis, Project Director at Oxford Innovation claims that:

> "Key UK organisations often commit to major programmes mentoring their senior personnel, but the role can be poorly supported. Despite major investment the results can be disappointing or even destructive – wasting potential which we, as a country, cannot afford to do. High potential individuals and teams achieve more through well-supported, well-thought through programmes."

Within this broad aim to create higher quality mentoring and coaching provision in the region, Oxford Innovation selected and recruited experienced executive coaches. The executive coach's primary aim was to upskill the fast growing business owners capacity to develop leaders and sustain high levels of growth, particularly at a time of austerity, when training budgets were under pressure. LeaderShape's approach was to encourage the development of the right mindset, recognising that the best mentors learn to act as a catalyst for change: they are flexible, understand the importance of personal chemistry, take time to build up the relationship and manage expectations. This was an approach that directly addressed the leadership challenges highlighted in a recent Chartered Institute of Personnel and Development (CIPD) report, where only half of directors and senior personnel from major blue chip and public sector firms believed their managers were equipped to tackle the current challenges of talent retention and development.

Deepening Learning and Impact through University Accreditation

LeaderShape's approach had a track record for impact, but it realised that university accreditation could add an additional level to their own delivery – in terms of the assessment, validation and hence recognition of the high level of skills and knowledge the coach-mentors would develop through their training. Yet LeaderShape also wanted to ensure that the approach to accreditation was flexible enough to meet their own delivery style, expertise and aspirations. LeaderShape approached and chose the University of Chester's Centre for Work Related Studies because of its philosophy towards personal transformation through experiential and work based learning, and its flexibility in accreditation (a radical approach described by Boud and Solomon and Symes (2001) and Wall (2010)). University accreditation was important to LeaderShape's customers because of the additional kudos and prestige offered by university accredited qualifications in an increasingly challenging marketplace.

The Postgraduate Certificate in Coach-Mentoring and Facilitation in Organisations was developed jointly as the first accredited programme for the Oxford Innovation coach-mentors, to act as competent facilitators enabling companies to develop high quality training and development programmes which boost their ability to develop leaders in-house when budgets are under pressure. The Postgraduate Certificate was designed by LeaderShape and the University of Chester as three training experiences (or modules):

- Principles, processes and skills of coaching

- Action learning facilitation

- Negotiated experiential learning.

The first two of these modules fine tunes the experienced coach-mentors' skills and knowledge around mentoring, coaching and the facilitating of action learning, and the third provides an opportunity for the coach-mentor to explore an area of practice which is important to their own professional needs, interests and aspirations. For example, some mentors are exploring, testing and evaluating new strategic management tools to support the development of small-enterprise managing directors, and others are exploring how they need to best respond to gender in their facilitation, all of which are in order to maximise business growth. It was important to LeaderShape to have a delivery and assessment design that supported their participants to reflect on and develop their own practice and skills.

Accreditation Processes and Relationship

LeaderShape worked with the University of Chester Centre for Work Related Studies, a recognised leader in work based learning and its accreditation, with over 1,000 learners on negotiated work based learning pathways and specialist expertise in leadership, facilitation and coaching. The Centre operates the University's flexible, negotiated work based learning framework which provides one of the most efficient and effective ways to design and accredit programmes for corporate or training provision with clients like LeaderShape (called the 'Work Based & Integrated Studies' framework). LeaderShape appointed one of its Directors as the academic lead, who worked very closely with a senior academic-practitioner (Client Advisor) at the Centre for Work Related Studies to develop the programme. Though LeaderShape had its own intellectual property around its delivery materials and ideas, it was still able to adopt some accredited modules that the Centre for Work Related Studies had already developed for its own flexible delivery. Its approach was similar to the University's and the modules were written flexibly.

In addition to this development work, the set-up of the Postgraduate Certificate involved:

- The University scrutinising and approving LeaderShape's proposed programme through a short proposal document

- The University scrutinising and approving LeaderShape facilitators as Associate Tutors of the University through Curriculum Vitaes

- The University providing initial training to LeaderShape's Associate Tutors covering how to design, facilitate and assess work based learning at university levels

- LeaderShape facilitators registering and starting the Postgraduate Certificate in Work Based Learning Facilitation generating a deeper understanding of how to design, facilitate and assess work based learning (and which leads towards Fellowship professional status of the Higher Education Academy)

Beyond the set-up of the Postgraduate Certificate, the on-going 'co-delivery' arrangement was as follows:

- LeaderShape's facilitators deliver the leadership, coaching, mentoring and facilitation content using a blend of direct instruction, interactive face-to-face activities, guided remote activities, guided and independent reading and remote coaching

- LeaderShape's facilitators assess the work of their training participants (students) allocating a grade and writing constructive and challenging feedback

- LeaderShape's facilitators check consistency of their own assessments

- LeaderShape's facilitators establish assessment guidance in line with University standards, and develop over time, based on feedback from their participants

- The University's Client Advisor quality assures the work for standards and consistency which may involve discussions around the feedback and mark given for work

- The University's Client Advisor works collaboratively with LeaderShape to develop enhancements to the provision and the design of the awards, and develop new provision

- The University arranges for external scrutiny of the work produced by LeaderShape participants, in order to ensure consistency and comparability across the University's awards and against national standards.

Through the quality assurance processes, the University was impressed with the quality of feedback and marking that LeaderShape provided: the quality of the formative and summative feedback was exemplary and the marks awarded were consistent and comparable to other awards. LeaderShape also actively sought feedback to refine and enhance the student experience, particularly the guidance offered to students about how to critically and creatively reflect on their practice. Two specific examples demonstrate this in two areas of detail that mattered to the participants.

The first example related to developing guidance around critically and creatively reflecting on own coaching and mentoring practice. LeaderShape found that the approach of traditional undergraduate (or even some other postgraduate studies) had established an expectation of what 'academic study' was where describing and analysing text book theory may have been sufficient. LeaderShape was able to clarify the importance of work based learning (and particularly developing mentoring/coaching practices), and how this distinctive approach involved being critical and creative about one's own practices, through becoming aware of the theories we use in practice, questioning them, and questioning ourselves as we engage in that practice. There was common ground between LeaderShape and the University that formed the foundation of rigorous study leading to deeper, longer-lasting learning and 'mastery' (at Master's-level) of coaching and mentoring practices in line with creating the consistency that Oxford Innovation needed.

The second example related to responding to a positive desire from participants to greater explore their learning and insight in assessed work. As LeaderShape's participants were very experienced professionals interested in generating new learning and insight, they also fed back the importance of not feeling constrained by a 'word count' limit for reflective reports about their developing coaching practices. At the same time, Leader*Shape* was appreciative of others in the same participant group who preferred word count limits, as they help focus attention during the time they did have committed to their studies (they were all busy practitioners with strict targets and deadlines). Leader*Shape* and the University quickly agreed assessment choices, and communicated these along with guidance, all of which still sat comfortably within the University's standard quality assurance systems, because of the flexible way in which the modules were designed, and because of the flexible policies of the Centre for Work Related Studies. Successfully working through this participant feedback in both cases was essential in building trust between the University and Leader*Shape*, in terms of confirming the quality of the student experience (and commitment to it), and the responsiveness and flexibility of the University to help Leader*Shape* achieve its particular outcomes.

Outcomes: Learning, Growth and New Practitioner Learning Journeys

The programme was designed to be a rigorous learning experience which is personally and professionally challenging, initially for the first cohort of 20 executive coach-mentors in Cornwall. It has proven to be a challenging experience for the cohort, and Leader*Shape* has continued to refine and enhance its delivery to meet the needs of the wider project. The radical work based learning approach has questioned practices and developed new facilitation and coaching competence within the cohort and there is growing evidence that this learning has impacted the small enterprises in Cornwall. Some of the initial evidence of the impact of the accredited training includes the small business owner-managers developing and implementing new marketing and/or growth strategies, increased sales and profit goals, identification and resolution of barriers to achieving these goals, increased levels of confidence and motivation towards reaching these goals, and increased sales and profits even in economic downturn. Because of such a positive experience, some of the Oxford Innovation coach-mentors expressed a real desire to continue to develop and refine their coaching and facilitation practice with Leader*Shape*, and so Leader*Shape* decided to explore additional, larger qualifications to support this, namely the Postgraduate Diploma (an additional 60 credits for those with the Postgraduate Certificate).

At the same time, Leader*Shape* had been finalising their intellectual property around an innovative and unique approach to developing transpersonal leadership behaviours (Knights, forthcoming). This was expressed as a work based learning journey through Emotionally Intelligent Leadership and Transpersonal Leadership. LeaderShape worked closely with the Client Advisor to accredit these journeys and a variety of new training experiences which would appeal to the Oxford Innovation cohort, and the large network of experienced professionals that had experienced and benefited from LeaderShape training and development in the past. LeaderShape saw this as a very important part of the community of practice they wanted to create for their expert network of executive coaches and facilitators nationally. Rather than having to design and offer multiple Diplomas, the Client Advisor enabled LeaderShape to offer their own negotiated work based learning Postgraduate Certificates and Diplomas, which could include both the training that the University had already approved plus the newly accredited Emotionally Intelligent and Transpersonal Leadership training. This meant LeaderShape could respond swiftly to the demands of their individual professionals and organisational clients alike, without the need to spend more time on designing and getting University approval for new provision as it arose. In addition, LeaderShape are exploring more ways to accredit shorter, bite-sized chunks of training and learning in areas of interest and importance to their thriving community of practice.

Lessons Learned

- It is important for the university and the training provider to work closely, openly and regularly to meet the needs of, and to appropriately challenge, well-qualified, highly experienced professionals

- It is useful to start with a specific and manageable product with a clearly defined remit. This manages risk and enables the training provider to become familiar with the particular systems and standards of the University

- Beyond initial products, a greater range can be developed towards the strategic aspirations of both organisations. It is important to be able to respond to the particular aspirations of the training provider which may mean creating new solutions

- It is important for both the university and the training provider to be committed to the same outcomes. In this case, both believed in the importance of personal transformation through work based learning, and the outcomes required for university level accreditation

- It is important to listen to participants to refine and develop practices. In this case, refinements in participant guidance helped the participants better engage with the training and the assessment of competence

- It is difficult to predict how participants will react or engage within training provision so it is important to listen and be flexible enough to adjust swiftly, which might mean writing learning outcomes more broadly or generically

- A negotiated flexible learning framework enables the university to work flexibly with a training provider to adjust provision according to the needs of the participant groups, and according to the needs of new clients of the training provider

- Enabling the training provider to operate negotiated flexible work based learning framework enables them the flexibility to react to and create new opportunities, though it is important that they are clear how they can use it, and that they are skilled in negotiating pathways and training experiences.

References

Boud, D. and Solomon, N. and Symes, C. (2001) New Practices for New Times, in Boud, D. and Solomon, N. (Eds) *Work-based Learning: A New Higher Education?*, Buckingham: Open University Press and the Society for Higher Education Research.

Knights, J. (forthcoming) The Invisible Elephant and The Pyramid Treasure (forthcoming).

Wall, T. (2010) University models for work based learning validation, in Roodhouse, S. and Mumford, J. (Eds) *Understanding Work Based Learning* (Farnham: Gower) pp41–54.

CHAPTER 8

Transforming Leadership, Learning and Life through Work Based Learning

Tony Wall*, Senior Lecturer and Principal Investigator, Centre for Work Related Studies, University of Chester

Jane Douglas, Director, Learning to Inspire UK

Jo Lord, Director, Learning to Inspire UK

Executive Summary

Learning to Inspire is a national, leading learning and development company based in the UK. It makes a positive difference through the development of individuals, teams and organisations, and is built on a passion for learning. It specialises in the applications of neuro-linguistic programming ideas to leadership, learning and life (see Learning to Inspire's website at learningtoinspire.co.uk), and is accredited by the Association for Neuro-Linguistic Programming (ANLP). Learning to Inspire worked with the University of Chester to accredit their internationally recognised Certified Practitioner in Neuro-Linguistic Programming, through various Professional Certificates and a Foundation Degree. Over time, this grew to include a Graduate Certificate in the Art of Leadership, a unique BA (Hons) degree, and more flexible provision which enables Learning to Inspire to respond to their own customers development needs, and more promotional 'taster' activities.

This case study highlights the following:

- Benefits of getting a well-regarded offer to a marketplace at the right price and time

---

- A range of accreditation options are useful to respond to different opportunities within a commercial marketplace particularly in times of economic difficulty

- Complexities can arise when additional government projects (and monitoring) are involved and it is useful to explore how to integrate and streamline these as far as possible

- Importance of including practical competence development of training in addition to applied knowledge within the academic assessment of learning and having a shared understanding of this

- Predicting the most appropriate 'university level' to design corporate programmes up front (in a way which motivates and hence enhances performance) can be difficult but being able to respond positively is crucial

- A negotiated flexible learning framework enables the university to work flexibly with a training provider to swiftly develop new provision according to the needs of the training provider and their clients

- Enabling the training provider to operate negotiated flexible work based learning framework enables them the flexibility to react to and create new opportunities and it is important to demonstrate how it can be fully exploited for commercial benefit.

Applying Transforming Ideas to Leadership, Learning and Life

Learning to Inspire work with ideas, tools and processes that enable personal and organisational development, often referred to as Neuro-Linguistic Programming (co-created by John Grinder and Richard Bandler). The Association for Neuro-Linguistic Programming define it as looking:

> '...at the way in which we think and process our thoughts (**Neuro**), the language patterns we use (**Linguistic**) and our behaviours (**Programming**) and how these interact to have a positive (or negative) effect on us as individuals (ANLP, 2011).'

Within the field, the 'Certified Practitioner' award has become an internationally recognised qualification for professionals who demonstrate competence in the knowledge and application of Neuro-Linguistic Programming ideas and processes. Learning to Inspire's Certified Practitioner was (and continues to be) a popular choice nationally, and was already accredited by the Association for Neuro-Linguistic Programming. Learning to Inspire realised that university level accreditation could add to the value proposition of their Certified Practitioner, making it even more distinctive, though recognising that not *all* of their customers would necessarily need or want it. A crucial factor for Learning to Inspire was that the structure and price had to be appropriate for their customer base, which included many small enterprises in England and Wales. The Certified Practitioner therefore provided the starting point for the core structure of the university accreditation.

In terms of price, Learning to Inspire was able to offer a market favourable rate through a major Employer Engagement project at the University. Curriculum developers (within the Employer Engagement team) together with senior academic-practitioners within the University's Centre for Work Related Studies, worked with Learning to Inspire to translate their training into university modules and short awards and helped them work through the University's quality processes. The University's Centre for Work Related Studies, a recognised leader in work based learning and its accreditation, leads the University's flexible, negotiated work based learning framework which provides one of the most efficient and effective ways to design and accredit programmes for corporate or training provision with clients like Learning to Inspire. It uses an innovative framework called the 'Work Based & Integrated Studies' framework (see Boud, Solomon and Symes (2001) and Wall (2010) for further examples).

In terms of structure, Learning to Inspire knew their customers well, and knew that working in smaller learning chunks would be more motivational and had a higher value proposition than much longer awards which smaller businesses may not initially see the full value in, but they were confident, from many years of experience, that once participants had experienced the real impacts within the business, that their customers would continue to buy their training products. The structure of the award was designed as four Professional Certificates (3 x 20 credits each), as outlined below. It was important to Learning to Inspire to develop and capture both practical competence in the processes and techniques in the assessment, so their participants would not be over-burdened with writing (rather than doing). This was fundamentally important to Learning to Inspire's philosophy of learning. It was agreed that the practical competence parts of each module would constitute 60% of each module assessment, the other 40% would normally be a written critical/creative reflection to consolidate and deepen that learning. The University's processes were sufficiently flexible to support this balance.

Professional Certificate in NLP as a Psychological Application in Leadership

- Self Awareness
- Relationship Awareness
- Transformational Leadership

Professional Certificate in NLP as a Psychological Application in Learning & Development

- Learner Engagement and Motivation
- Designing Learning Programmes
- Facilitation Skills

Professional Certificate in NLP as a Psychological Application in Coaching

- Guiding and Mentoring
- Teaching and Coaching
- Sponsoring and Awakening

Professional Certificate in NLP as a Psychological Application in Life Mastery

- Introduction to AQAL (All Quadrants All Levels)
- Exploring Self
- Life Practices

In addition to these short awards, those learners who successfully engaged in the modules of the first two Professional Certificates and wanted to end their studies at that point, could be awarded as a Certificate of Higher Education in Applied NLP in Personal and Organisational Development and if the practitioners completed all of the modules successfully, they were awarded a Foundation Degree in Applied Neuro-Linguistic Programming in Personal and Organisational Development. Testament to the quality of Learning to Inspire's training and impact, participant motivation and commitment, and the overall proposition, most practitioners progressed impressively through the Professional Certificates and the Foundation Degree.

A Relationship Supporting High Quality Learning and Standards

Learning to Inspire worked with Employer Engagement curriculum developers and senior academic-practitioners within the University's Centre for Work Related Studies, to initially set up the above awards, which involved:

- The University scrutinising and approving Learning to Inspire's proposed awards through short proposal documents

- The University scrutinising and approving Learning to Inspire's facilitators as Associate Tutors of the University through Curriculum Vitaes

- The University providing initial training to Learning to Inspire's Associate Tutors covering how to design, facilitate and assess work based learning at university levels

- Learning to Inspire's facilitators registering and starting the Postgraduate Certificate in Work Based Learning Facilitation generating a deeper understanding of how to design, facilitate and assess work based learning (and which leads towards Fellowship professional status of the Higher Education Academy)

Beyond the set-up of the awards, the on-going 'co-delivery' arrangement with the University's Centre for Work Related Studies was as follows:

- Learning to Inspire's facilitators deliver the training content using a blend of highly interactive face-to-face training, guided remote activities, guided and independent reading and remote coaching

- Learning to Inspire's facilitators assess the work of their training participants (students) allocating a grade and writing constructive and challenging feedback

- Learning to Inspire's facilitators establish assessment guidance in line with University standards, and develop over time, based on feedback from their participants

- The University's Client Advisor quality assures the work for standards and consistency which may involve discussions around the feedback and mark given for work

- The University's Client Advisor works collaboratively with Learning to Inspire to develop enhancements to the provision and the design of the awards, and develop new provision

- The University arranges for external scrutiny of the work produced by Learning to Inspire's participants, in order to ensure consistency and comparability across the University's awards and against national standards

Outcomes: Learning, New Options and Learning Journeys

As the award titles suggest, the training provision at Learning to Inspire was designed to transform leadership, learning and life and continues to have a strong and excellent reputation for this. Employees and their managers across England and Wales have changed perspectives in their lives and have taken major changes in their career and/or life direction. Many others have applied powerful techniques to achieve significant outcomes in their professional lives. Out of almost 100 students originally registered on Learning to Inspire awards, almost 40 are about to complete the Foundation Degree, and many expressed interest in progressing their studies through to a BA (Hons) degree. In order to serve this market, a new BA (Hons) degree Applied Neuro-Linguistic Programming was developed, which closely resembled the neuro-linguistic programming 'Certified Master Practitioner' (the more advanced progression from the Certified Practitioner course). This is a unique degree, and is the first in the UK to achieve accreditation by the Association for Neuro-Linguistic Programming. The Client Advisor also arranged for Learning to Inspire to be able to negotiate awards swiftly for their rapidly growing network of Certified Practitioners across the UK, in order to continue to serve their needs over time.

As part of the BA (Hons) awards, the Client Advisor worked with the facilitators to develop specific marking criteria, and innovative approaches to assessment, including negotiating learning outcomes with individuals, and patchwork and portfolio assessments. Learning to Inspire particularly wanted to offer participants greater opportunities for professional learning and insight, and was keen to explore and experiment with such approaches. One example was the use of the patchwork assessment approach, a tried and tested alternative to traditional academic essays with proven effects on engagement and learning. The patchwork approach enables small training activities ('patches') to form the assessment of a participant's module, and is brought ('stitched') together and deepened through a critical/creative reflection. This approach also demonstrated how Learning to Inspire could develop and deliver smaller chunks of learning over time to form a module, say taster sessions for their own potential or new customers.

A more strategic development was to enable Learning to Inspire to offer customised awards to their own corporate clients, such as a Graduate Certificate in the Art of Leadership, which involved three modules: Leading Self, Leading Others, Leading in Organisations. One of Learning to Inspire's clients for a customised award had an organisational culture and environment that did not facilitate the fresh, radical and creative thinking that the training was attempting to promote and encourage, certainly at this 'graduate level'. Learning to Inspire's facilitators persisted to facilitate and support the participants in the organisation, and although it was initially uncomfortable for some learners, these learners did broaden their perspectives and realise the benefits of the transformational ideas and processes offered. It was difficult to predict, up front, how these learners would react to and engage in this 'graduate level' training at the design stage, but Learning to Inspire's positive response was beneficial for their client, for itself, and for maintaining the standards of the University. The Client Advisor at the University's Centre for Work Related Studies provided on-going advice and support to Learning to Inspire to ensure standards were appropriate and that the participants were given additional advice and support where necessary.

As the economic down-turn increasingly hit Learning to Inspire's client base (many of which are small enterprises), Learning to Inspire needed to find a way to retain the value-added of the university accreditation at a price that was affordable to the increasingly price sensitive marketplace. Learning to Inspire was able to work with the University's Centre for Work Related Studies to introduce a 'credit-rating' version of the 'Certified Practitioner' in addition to the 'co-delivery' version described above. Though co-delivery allowed Learning to Inspire to deliver full university awards (e.g. Professional Certificate, Foundation Degree), 'credit-rating' did not. For those participants who did want to progress with a university award, they would register with the University and then 'import' the training with a given credit level and value (180 credits: 120 at level 4, 60 credits at level 5). This was a trade-off Learning to Inspire considered to be appropriate for the new economic climate. It was a less intensive process, as Learning to Inspire facilitators did not need to attach grades or detailed feedback as before. As the 'credit-rating' option did not link with the Employer Engagement project, it meant that the administrative systems associated with the project were much simpler and more efficient. Overall, it offered the best value to Learning to Inspire and their customers during the economic crunch.

Lessons Learned

- UK Government funding enabled Learning to Inspire and the University of Chester to provide a commercially well regarded offer at the right price to Learning to Inspire customers and this was important in the initial sales and recruitment success of the offer to a variety of sectors and sizes of organisation

- At the same time, the on-going sales potential of the offer was limited by the limited timing of UK Government funding. The 'standard' pricing model applied to the price sensitive marketplace meant that the value proposition in a time of austerity was less compelling

- Within this context, it was important to be able to offer other accreditation options (i.e. credit-rating rather than co-delivering) for Learning to Inspire's training, which provided a much more cost-effective route to university accreditation. Though not providing the same offer, it provided an alternative offer, which would benefit both Learning to Inspire and the University of Chester

- It can be important to include the practical competence development aspects of training in addition to applied knowledge within the academic assessment of participant learning and have a shared understanding of this

- It can be difficult to predict the most appropriate 'university level' to design corporate programmes up front (in a way which motivates and hence enhances performance), but it is important to be responsive and positive, developing additional support and guidance as and when required, towards the original desired outcome

- A negotiated flexible learning framework enables the university to work flexibly with a training provider to swiftly develop new provision according to the needs of the training provider and their clients

- Enabling the training provider to operate negotiated flexible work based learning framework allows them the flexibility to react to and create new opportunities, which is important in demonstrating how it can be fully exploited for commercial benefit.

References

ANLP Association of Neuro-Linguistic Programming (2011) *What is NLP?*, available at http://www.anlp.org/what-is-nlp, accessed 20th April.

Boud, D. and Solomon, N. and Symes, C. (2001) New Practices for New Times, in Boud, D. and Solomon, N. (Eds) *Work-based Learning: A New Higher Education?* (Buckingham: Open University Press and the Society for Higher Education Research).

Wall, T. (2010) University models for work based learning validation, in Roodhouse, S. and Mumford, J. (Eds) *Understanding Work Based Learning* (Farnham: Gower) pp41–54.

CHAPTER 9

Work Based Learning for Community Cohesion Training in the Social Housing Sector

Renata Eyres, Karen Harrison, Maureen McMahon and Ruth Potts, University of Salford

Sadia Akram, Oldham Housing Investment Partnership

Executive Summary

This case study presents lessons learnt from critical reflection upon the development and implementation of a responsive Work Based Learning (WBL) module, designed in partnership with the social housing sector. The aim of the project was to enable employees of the social housing sector to implement, reflect on, and evaluate the knowledge, skills, and experiences gained from a community cohesion training programme through focusing on a work related activity. As a result, action plans to meet future learning needs aimed at improving practice, were developed by each student.

This case study highlights:

- Having dedicated relationship management resources is important for building and maintaining a strong relationship and a high level of trust between the university and the employer

- A tri-partite learning agreement can accommodate the needs and requirements of the learner, the employer and the university. This must be reviewed to identify student progression, barriers and/or difficulties

- The integration of work based learning in partnership with employers can enable both students and employers to benefit from focusing on a work related activity in order to evaluate their knowledge and skills and to reflect on their experiences in order to improve practice

- Pre-entry student profiling enables the correct level of study to be identified, and to support the initial negotiation of an individual learning plan

- Negotiated delivery, the use of a blended learning approach and student profiling allow students with different learning styles to identify and select the most appropriate format for their individual learning

Introduction

In 2001 parts of the North West of England experienced severe community tensions on a scale not seen since the riots of 1991. Subsequent government policies have focused on promoting shared values and a celebration of diversity to encourage community cohesion. One outcome of this impetus has been employer investment in community cohesion training to underpin best practice. Within this context, Oldham Housing Investment Partnership (OHIP) developed and ran an in-house training programme, which concentrated on issues relating to community cohesion. OHIP is the umbrella organisation for a number of different partnership organisations in the Social Housing Sector across the North West.

The University of Salford was approached by OHIP due to its regional and national reputation for the provision of education and training in the areas of social care, housing and regeneration. This was with a view to formally recognise the community cohesion training programme by awarding higher education (HE) credit for the learning and practice development. As a result, the training component was enhanced and enabled the practitioners to reflect upon, and evaluate, the impact of their new knowledge, skills and experiences on their individual practice.

In April 2009, staff from the Business Services Unit (BSU) at the University of Salford met with colleagues from OHIP to discuss the development of a WBL module specifically for OHIP employees. Potential students were selected by the employers to undertake the module, all of whom held diverse roles, all with varying backgrounds and levels of experience within the organisation. The only common denominator was that each student had taken part in the 'in-house' Community Cohesion training programme. OHIP wanted to assess the effectiveness of the 'in-house' training but importantly the intention was to demonstrate that the Community Cohesion Training was being embedded within their practice. The use of the Work Based Learning Framework at the University of Salford provided a range of Work Based Learning modules that would facilitate student learning and help provide them with the knowledge and skills to evaluate the impact of the application of the Community Cohesion Training. This resulted in the employer being prepared to invest further in staff development. Staff could now clearly demonstrate how they were utilising the training programme. Specifically, they could now provide a range of evidence to support the positive impact that the training had made, and a demonstrable impact on their own confidence in their ability to make a significant difference in the communities within which they work.

Each student completed a pre-entry profiling exercise in advance of starting the module, which was in the form of a self-assessment tool. This enabled the students to identify:

- How they could apply the training
- How the organisation might benefit
- What they each needed to do in order to move forward

Due to the diverse backgrounds and experiences of the students, it was decided to deliver the module at different academic levels (which represented different levels of challenge for the practitioners). Delivering at two different levels to one cohort facilitated shared induction, group tutorials, and master classes. Individual tutorials enabled students to focus specifically on their needs and the relevant academic level.

To meet the needs of both the employer and the student the programme team agreed the dates and locations of each of the sessions to be delivered. The induction and the assessment sessions were held at the University of Salford, and all of the individual surgery and group tutorial sessions were held off campus at one of the OHIP sites. Conducting these sessions at the employers' site emphasised that both locations were sites of learning, and highlighted the benefits to the employer of investing in Work Based Learning. In this case, the benefits included employees valuing the work place as a learning environment, there was minimal disruption to employee working time, it made higher education accessible to this group of practitioners and because of the employer's investment in them, staff felt valued by the employer.

In order to ensure a mutual understanding, the roles and responsibilities of staff involved in the delivery of the module from both the University and the employer were agreed at the outset. For example, the arrangements for Personal Tutoring and the employer-based learner guide/mentor ensured that the expectations of the employers were clearly agreed and defined very early on. This also promoted a better understanding of requirements, for example, site delivery and time planning with the student, taking account of their individual job requirements. Mentor training and support was identified and implemented in order to maximise the support for student learning and those supporting that learning.

It was vitally important that a close collaborative working partnership and clear lines of communication were in place to ensure that any problems arising throughout the programme could be dealt with quickly and effectively by the most appropriate person. It takes a great deal of time and effort from both parties to develop a level of trust and open and honest communication. It was therefore imperative from the outset that the University managed the expectations of the employer and did not promise to deliver unrealistic outcomes. The team at the University's BSU have found that employers want to develop long-term relationships rather than single transactions, and that this is more likely to happen if both parties are clear about what they can expect from each other, and what specific actions are necessary to achieve that expectation. In particular, this included selecting and negotiating appropriate work based activities, participation in on-going development meetings, ensuring students were provided with the necessary support in the workplace, discussing timeframes and sharing information with the employer to deal with any issues as they arose. Actively participating in the evaluation gave the employer an important stakeholder contribution and information for future action planning involving Work Based Learning.

Evaluation

A qualitative and quantitative evaluation was undertaken at the end of the module, which incorporated the views of the students, employers, external examiner and the Work Based Learning facilitators. The intention of the evaluation was to:

- Determine if students could evidence implementation of the community cohesion training to their individual practice
- Identify trends, emerging themes and issues from the data
- Make recommendations and identify actions for improvement for subsequent intakes
- Recognise areas of good practice, promote 'good news' and to inform the ongoing development of the work based learning framework
- Inform future partnership working

Examples of Student Comments:

'enjoyed learning about my learning style and where I can improve my skills'

'Reflecting on where you are now and using that to make changes is a positive experience.'

'Enjoyed this kind of environment and would if given the opportunity continue my learning on a full HE programme.'

Employer comment: 'Amazed that our idea of getting training accredited by the University of Salford has worked and been so passionately embraced.'

Key points from the evaluation can be summarised as follows:

For learners:

> Students were pleased with the WBL module and they were able to evidence the application of community cohesion training to the development of their role

> Students welcomed the chance to 'reflect on their own learning' and appreciated the opportunity to work with and learn from colleagues from across OHIP

> Students valued the support given and the blended learning approach, which enhanced their positive learning experience at the University of Salford

> Collaborative relationships with both facilitators and work place learner guide/mentors (who had been prepared in advance) were reported as positive, with students saying they felt 'well supported' by the University

> Students felt that they had opportunity to link theory to work related activities and develop as independent learners

> Students could evidence how the work based training had impacted positively on their roles by applying theory to practice

For OHIP:

> The responses from OHIP managers were equally positive and they welcomed the opportunities presented to support their staff and the flexible approach to teaching and learning which fitted well with students' work commitments

> The employers appreciated that having a clearly defined timeframe with the student was an important factor

For University staff and external reviewers:

> The external examiner's feedback was very favourable and included comments such as

'This is a sensible and thoughtful approach to developing this area of provision. The team showed a clear understanding of the challenges involved and future developments are very promising'

and

'I am looking forward to strengthening our relationship and hope to be able to share good practice with the team where we can learn from each other as the programme expands'

➢ The work based learning facilitators commented that pre-entry profiling was a vital component for the preparation of both the student and the employer for HE study

➢ It was a reciprocal learning process although key emphasis was on employer ownership and in determining the most appropriate timeframe and resource requirements within the work context

➢ Effective communication between all key stakeholders was considered to be a critical factor

Figure 9.1: WBL Process in summary

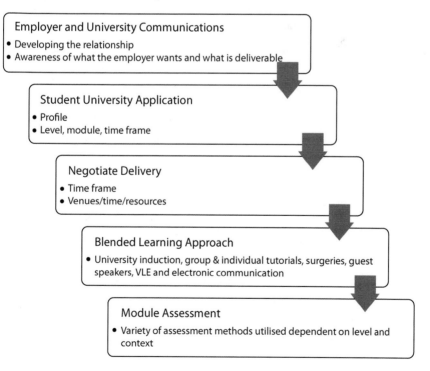

Impact

On completion of the Work Based Learning module, the evaluation demonstrated that the students had developed a deeper understanding, and an appreciation of their role and responsibilities in OHIP and the wider social housing sector. This was demonstrated both from the content of their portfolios submitted and from feedback from the evaluations that were undertaken. It enabled the sharing of good practice across the partnership and provided opportunities to discuss relevant issues that have an influence on the social housing sector within the local and wider community.

Focussing on a specific work related activity was directly linked to the individual student's appraisal and career aspirations and continuing personal and professional development. This allowed them to further develop their knowledge and skills as well as develop a positive attitude towards independent learning and reflective practice. Undertaking this study changed their perceptions of Higher Education, as something which was outside of their grasp, and enabled them to recognise their capability to study at a higher level. It boosted their confidence, and being awarded academic credit endorsed the value of their learning and development.

Recommendations and Actions Drawn from the Evaluation

- Pre-entry negotiations need to include timeframes

- The employer needs to develop understanding of the Work Based Learning modules and the roles and responsibilities of those involved

- Partners need to identify resources for study, including geographical locations

- Ensure that expectations of managers in the employing organisation(s) are clearly articulated

- Ensure students are fully aware of what is expected of them by utilising the pre registration individual profile, to include module content summary; expected time commitment; benefits to student (application of learning); progression; number of tutorials and where these will be delivered

- A clear evaluation plan with identified responsibilities should be agreed at the time of contract exchange. All parties should be clear about what is expected, the trigger points for evaluative activity throughout the module duration, how feedback will be collated, who it will be circulated by and how it will be used to inform development (or respond instantly to specific problems)

- It is vitally important that both the students and employers are aware of the ethical implications of using their organisational data and the need to maintain client confidentiality when producing evidence for assessment within their portfolios or presentations. They must adhere to Data Protection legislation and research governance criteria should be applied when utilising data that has originally been collected for one purpose, then being used in other work

Lessons Learned

The emergent learning from experience illustrates the importance of partnership working between the employer and University, and effective communication. A strong relationship and a high level of trust between the University and the employer are essential when working in partnership, and this can be maintained by having dedicated relationship management resources. Use of a tri-partite learning agreement can accommodate the needs and requirements of the learner, the employer and the University. Review must take place on a regular basis identifying student progression, barriers and/or difficulties, which **may** hinder students or prevent them achieving the planned outcomes. A revised plan may then be agreed by all three parties' concerned and additional support given if required.

The integration of Work Based Learning in partnership with employers can enable both students and employers to benefit from focusing on a work-related activity in order to evaluate their knowledge and skills and to reflect on their experiences in order to improve practice. This process can enhance a student's confidence and competence to deliver improved practice and to engage with higher education. From the employers perspective investing in staff development demonstrates the value placed on staff and their commitment to develop and disseminate best practice. It not only supports the University's commitment to Widening Participation, but also provides the opportunity for effective knowledge transfer and future business collaboration.

Accurate pre-entry student profiling prior to commencing the module enables the correct level of study to be identified, and to support the initial negotiation of an individual learning plan. In particular, it helps define specific learning outcomes and types of evidence suitable for assessment. In addition, negotiated delivery, the use of a blended learning approach and student profiling allow students with different learning styles to identify and select the most appropriate format for their individual learning.

CHAPTER 10

On the Move – the Impact of Management Development at P&O North Sea Ferries

Richard Shaw, P&O Route Manager

David Godfrey, Product Development Manager, The Hull College Group

Executive Summary

This case study highlights the following:

- The benefits of designing flexible training programmes that meet with the needs of a fast moving business environment

- How developing an open and honest relationship between the provider and the client produces a mutually rewarding learning environment

- The importance of a progressive training programme that allows learners to aspire to unexpected levels of achievement

- How wide ranging training options adds value to training interventions.

- How further and higher education can be linked to provide training solutions that are cohesive and cover all levels within an organisation

- How the importance of being able to offer solutions to business problems is an important feature of training programmes

The Partnership

The Hull College Group is an organisation comprised of Hull College, Goole College, Harrogate College and Harrogate International Business School. The aim of the above is to work with employers to deliver training that is based around the needs of business and that is progressive It was with this remit that the group entered into a partnership with P&O North Sea Ferries in 2003.

In many ways a major ferry operation can be seen has both a floating hotel and one large planning problem. There is an endless list of things that have to be planned: crews, cabin reservations, freight, cars, maintenance, food outlets, shops, luggage, manifests, equipment and passenger welfare. Each problem has its own considerations, complexities, targets and time horizons but all are interrelated.

This case study highlights the following:

- The benefits of designing flexible training programmes that meet with the needs of a fast moving business environment

- How developing an open and honest relationship between the provider and the client produces a mutually rewarding learning environment

- The importance of a progressive training programme that allows learners to aspire to unexpected levels of achievement

- How wide ranging training options adds value to training interventions

- How further and higher education can be linked to provide training solutions that are cohesive and cover all levels within an organisation

- How the importance of being able to offer solutions to business problems is an important feature of training programmes

The Link between NVQ and Degree Level Learning

It was against the above background that P&O approached Hull College in 2003 when they were seeking a training intervention. The importance of this intervention was that it should provide accredited training, be progressive and develop the skills of their employees. The added complication was that the training should cover all operations and that courses must cover all levels from 2 to 7 of, the then, National Qualifications framework. These levels reflected the degree of competence required within the job roles and their seniority within the staff structure.

It was therefore necessary to involve both technical training via NVQs but also an underpinning knowledge and understanding especially at levels 5 and 7 via the Higher Education route. It was agreed at the outset that the senior managers would require additional input and this was provided by various training interventions delivered via the staff of Harrogate International Business School. The main thrust of the training was to provide a platform for learners that would enable them to access degree level business courses. The courses most suitable for the above were those of the Chartered Management Institute. These courses in management and leadership provided the opportunity for the lecturers to base their assessments around the work of the learners and to encourage them to synthesise theory in such a way that the learning enabled them to provide solutions to various business problems.

Whilst the main aim at the outset was to develop managers it soon became apparent that other training interventions would be required such as retail, and customer service. These requirements were also included in the level 5 and 7 programmes. The main aim of the training was that it would allow learners to progress and to integrate this within the training programme. The link between the NVQ delivery and that of Higher Education was achieved via a carefully planned assessment of prior learning. This assessment took account of the ability demonstrated by the learner and mapped prior learning outcomes with those at a higher level.

Fitting Training to Business Needs

P&O North Sea Ferries sail out of the port of Hull to two North Sea destinations of Zeebrugge in Belgium and the Dutch port of Rotterdam. The routes are serviced by four ships, two of British ownership and two owned by the Dutch arm of P&O. Each and every day, except Christmas, these ships sail out of Hull and therefore they are in Hull or the European ports on alternate days.

The ferries provide a service for freight users and private cars each of which have their own requirements and level of service. The freight drivers have their own area of the ferry including restaurant and sleeping accommodation. The private passengers require a very high level of service and this is provided by various distinct operations.

The Food and Beverage team provide a service in respect of a four star al a carte restaurant, self service restaurant, snack bars, coffee lounge and various bars. The guest services team provide on board operations in respect of customer service, cabins and general hygiene. The retail team run three outlets, luxury goods, books and souvenirs and a liquor and wine store.

The ferries have differing capacities in respect of number of passengers they are able to carry. Two of the ships have a capacity of 700 passengers and the other two of over 1200. In addition to the above teams there is also the engineering operation which carries out general maintenance and the crew who actually steer and navigate the ships.

The competition for North Sea freight passengers is fierce and so it is necessary to provide a very high level of service. Innovation is called for in order to differentiate P&O from their competitors.

Each ship has a set of targets or Key Performance Indicators KPIs and these reports are filed each week with good natured rivalry between the ships, each seeking to be top of the 'leader board.'

The strategic impetus for the training was the need to respond to low staff morale, staff turnover and poor performance issues. The college were seeking to build on their growing reputation has a provider of excellent training that meet with the expectations of client organisations. This was in line with the funding streams; such as Train to Gain that had been introduced to provide support for the strategy to improve the skills of the UK workforce.

The perceived benefits were that operatives would have improved skills with accredited qualifications, that the qualifications required by staff in all posts would have job specifications that included the need to achieve the specific technical skill underpinned with a bona fide nationally recognised qualification.

The business development managers at the college met with senior managers of P&O and mapped out the various qualifications against the various job roles. This was then matched to funding and an action plan put in place for the delivery of the training. The traditional modes of delivery would not work as staff worked on shifts of two weeks duration and much of the training would have to be delivered at times that met with availability of the trainees. Much of the training therefore would have to be delivered at night and when the ferries were at sea. It was agreed that the first tranche of training would be for those in operations and team leading levels for managers. This decision was appropriate in that it was based on the need to provide cost efficient training and to role out the Train to Gain programme.

The quality assurance aspects of the training were at the forefront of the training strategy. The college had excellent QA procedures that had been recognised by Ofsted but this programme also had to address motivation of learners. We also built into the programme meetings to review progress and a support mechanism for all learners. This was an important feature of the training programme in that the aim of the training was that the learner journey would be one that was enjoyable and with a successful outcome.

It was agreed that the first staff to engage with the training would be the team leaders all of whom were enrolled an NVQs with underpinning delivery of knowledge and understanding. However, it soon become evident that whilst the team leaders were being put through their training programmes, those at higher levels of management also required training and indeed were in fact requesting this via their performance appraisals. Management and leadership therefore became the catalyst for training on all of the ferries. The strategy was agreed that if all senior managers engaged with the training then it would indeed set an example that the company were very serious about their intention to train all staff.

The most suitable training courses for senior managers would be those accredited by the Chartered Management Institute at NVQ levels 5 and 7. Although the NVQ would assess competence the knowledge and understanding would be addressed with the delivery of training sessions aimed at specific skills. These included ITC, finance, presentations and communication. Alongside the training the company had introduced KPIs on all ferries that set benchmarks in terms of profitability, operational efficiency, management of resources and innovation.

This was a real challenge for us to deal with in that the traditional role of the assessor would no longer be adequate. The new role called for an assessor with senior operational experience and the ability to act as an assessor, coach and mentor. A challenging set of skills but the tutor's role was of vital importance if the training programme was to be successful.

Each manager was interviewed by their tutor and the appropriate level of course identified to fit with both their managerial role and their ability to engage with the rigours of assessment. An individual action plan was produced for each learner with regular meetings arranged and progress very carefully monitored. It had been agreed at the outset that each learner would be given a target date by which they would be required to complete.

However, individual circumstances would be taken into account and if deemed necessary the timelines would be adjusted. The one to one meetings proved to be very successful as a number of issues came to light and individual needs identified. The meetings with learners would be centred on the units of the respective qualification. The learners in proving competence would agree a plan with their tutor with many interventions being made in respect of theory and techniques. The tutor would work with the learner to address operational issues and advise on the appropriate action or point the learner in the direction of helpful information. It become apparent as the training progressed that the approach taken was proving to be successful and that a new style of management was emerging. Each KPI was being addressed with enthusiasm and performance of senior managers and their teams began to improve. New procedures introduced as a result of the training were also welcomed, especially staff performance appraisals, held at regular intervals The findings of these meetings provided a fresh challenge for P&O and the college, as staff who had been left out of the current training programme were very keen to enrol on appropriate courses. This was welcomed by the college and proved that their approach of one to one delivery was providing the correct level of support and that learners were reacting positively.

Outcomes: The P&O Perspective

Historically in the Merchant Navy there were a significant number of managers/supervisors at all levels who have worked their way up through the system. Many of these individuals have no formal management training or qualifications, some had rather limited education and others had left the formal education system at the age of fourteen and went to sea school where they received training on catering and seamanship. These employees were in the age range of early forties to early fifties. It was anticipated that there would be a very strong reluctance by some to get involved in a learning programme. This reluctance being fuelled by apprehension and fear of possible failure, so P&O started a series of in-house activity based workshops and training aimed at improving communication and leadership behaviours. These workshops proved to be a success in terms of outcome and crucially removed the apprehension of learning, or relearning new things.

There was still those who were reluctant to embark on a learning programme, however once staff members started to interact with their assigned tutor from Hull College the programme began to gather its own momentum. Over time confidence in the process grew, meeting with tutors built confidence in the relationship in terms of support guidance and confidentiality. The impact of the new learning on the students very quickly became apparent. Contributions at meetings both formal and informal were clearly thought out and delivered with a new found confidence. Ideas that previously had just been mentioned in passing became owned action plans. At this point on board management started to involve the team leaders in the setting of and agreeing their own KPI's. This was a real success and signified that a change in approach, thinking and improved understanding of the role of a team leader had taken place. Communication in all directions improved dramatically, this had a real benefit in terms of productivity and interactions. Trust and confidence grew between all levels of the on board operation. Time spent on communication reduced, as the quality of communication improved.

The number of on board domestic issues which can be very complicated, as the crews live together for long periods, reduced as the leadership behaviour of the team leaders improved. The fact that more time was spent on directing/supervising staff meant that team leaders got to know their staff better. As a result morale improved to such an extent that you could feel a real difference in the atmosphere on board. An unintended and unforeseen benefit of the programme was that on board crew members came together to form a crew welfare committee that arranged social events and outings for crew. The crew even started to run a crew shop for day to day items only available in town. This resulted in a small profit which was invested in items for the crew, decided by the crew. The creation of the crew shop itself was used as evidence towards an NVQ.

The modular nature of the NVQ clearly helped the learners in that they could embark on a module at a time with clearly stated learning objectives per module. Initially the wording of some of the expected outcomes was difficult to understand for people who had been away from education for some time. Once the staff understood the wording they started to use the language and phraseology correctly during on board interactions. This demonstrated the understanding of these phrases/words and as a result when the team leaders/managers interacted with seniors within the company, or a representative of other companies, these interactions took on a more professional air.

As we had several individuals working through a variety of NVQ's their impact on the business started to become apparent. Various ideas and initiatives were, and continue to be, developed and introduced into many aspects of the operation. There were many noticeable successes, for example, previously we had information re the cost of our non productive stores (chemicals, cloths etc) usage but no on board management process. One was introduced and the result was a 30+% reduction in non productive costs over that financial year. There were several successes of this magnitude.

The most noticeable impact on the business was a joint project between P&O and Hull College involving the redesigning of the long standing work practises of how our 540 cabins were serviced on a daily basis. The additional benefits to learners was the opportunity to be involved in a project of this scale from its conception, the gathering of data, the interpretation of this data, then the implementation of a new work system based on the efficient use of available resources, essentially manpower. Again it is no coincidence that since the team leaders/managers and now front line staff have undertaken study the Pride of Hull has become the top performing ship in its class.

There are many individuals who were introduced or re introduced to learning through the partnership with Hull College and the NVQ programme who now continue to study privately. On board management are frequently asked through the performance review route about the possibility of studying for an NVQ, but not just an NVQ, individuals now do some research and frequently ask for specific NVQs. Personal development plans are very common at all levels on board which was unthinkable four years ago.

These outcomes are clear indications of how education has impacted on individuals in terms of re re-energising/motivating and re-engaging them, these individuals then deliver all these behaviours and attitudes to the benefit of the business to such a degree that a culture of continuous improvement is now present on board the vessel. As a result of our learning we now have improved systems for data collection, and have staff at several levels that can interpret this information into improvement action so that passengers service, cost management, and efficiency are improving all the time. As a result of our learning we now have the will and confidence to achieve these outcomes.

Conclusions

- UK Government funding enabled Hull College to deliver cost effective accredited training. It was important that learners achieved an outcome that was recognised via the QCF

- Training must be planned against business aims and objectives and tangible outcomes must be seen to of been accomplished by the provider

- Training intervention should be progressive with access for learners to higher levels made available if they a have the ability and desire to progress

- Assessment should be related to the learner's job role and business strategy thus enabling learners to demonstrate how they are using their learning to benefit the client organisation.

CHAPTER 11

The Pharmaceutical Industry Advanced Training Experience

John Collett, Chief Scientific Officer, Quay Pharma, Deeside

Professor Brian Lockwood, Director of PIAT, School of Pharmacy & Pharmaceutical Sciences, University of Manchester

Executive Summary

- The Pharmaceutical Industry Advanced Training (PIAT)programme was designed to fulfil specific Pharmaceutical training in academic subjects

- Involvement of a professional body, the Royal Pharmaceutical Society of Great Britain (RPSGB) in the initial stages brought the two parties, the Pharmaceutical Industry and the Higher Education Institutions (HEI) together

- Programme structure was established

- Expansion of programme was carried out, again after consultation with Pharma

Requirement for the Programme/Concept

Academic staff in UK Schools of Pharmacy routinely consult for the Pharmaceutical Industry, and all original tutors for the Industrial Pharmacy programme were either industrial pharmacists or UK academics. Careers fairs and undergraduate lectures are given by industrial pharmacists under the auspices of the Industrial Pharmacy Group of the RPSGB. Many academic staff have moved into Pharma as employees, and recently there has been a move in the opposite direction, accelerated by rationalisation in the industry. Cross fertilisation of this type reaps rewards for both sectors. Over many years Industry has recruited staff from either secondary or tertiary education without PhD level in pharmaceutical sciences or equivalent. Many of these employees have built up much experience in the industrial environment, but need further qualifications, obtainable only at a Higher Education Institute (HEI).

The concept of work placed learning was identified by the Industrial Pharmacy Group of the Pharmaceutical Society. A competitive bidding process was organised, and a bid from the then Department of Pharmacy in Manchester led by John Collett, was successful in 1989. The aim was to supply clearly identified training needs (resulting in 17 specific modular topics) for employees in the UK pharmaceutical industry, allowing qualifications up to the degree of MSc to be awarded. The most attractive feature of the scheme was the ability of employers to retain the services of their staff while studying for Pharmaceutical Industry Advanced Training (PIAT) qualifications, and this was the main point that "sold" the scheme to the Directors of ICI Pharmaceuticals, Smith Kline French, Glaxo and Burroughs Wellcome. All four agreed to help in the start up, with ICI offering the services of Dr Ray Longworth for a year and the others offering financial help. Ray Longworth started as the first Director, and with considerable help from John Fell of the Department of Pharmacy, put tremendous effort into promoting and administering the set up. The curriculum was planned in collaboration with major companies including Glaxo and ICI, and a combination of authors and tutors based in major Pharma from UK, US, Japan, Switzerland, Thailand and UK academia were appointed The first student entered the programme in 1989 and the first MSc graduate completed in 1995.

Course Structure and Modus Operandi

Originally there were eight modules, now there is a choice of 17 modules available in the Industrial Pharmacy Programme, covering virtually all aspects of pharmaceutical manufacturing and development. The modules have EU and US relevance, and are applicable worldwide due to the overriding importance of Food and Drug Administration (FDA) and European Medicine Agency (EMEA) regulations. The aims of the programme were to have a flexible structure of free standing modules. These have an open and distance learning style, allowing minimum time to be absent from the workplace, which benefits both employer and student. There are a range of entry options; a minimum of an HND is usually required for a Diploma, and a degree level scientific qualification is usually needed for an MSc, most students are science graduates. Over many years Industry has recruited staff from either secondary or tertiary education without PhD level in pharmaceutical sciences or equivalent. Many of these employees have built up much experience in the industrial environment, but need further qualifications, obtainable only at a HEI.

This prior learning is not quantifiable nor transferable into the programme as credited experience (APEL) at our institution*, but it does give recognition of the fact that students are fully aware of the concepts and practicalities of working in Pharma.

---

* This is standard practice in some institutions.

No prior learning (APL) is required for individual modules, but four credited PIAT modules with a pass mark of 50% equate to BSc equivalence.

Individual course modules have a workload of 150 hours per module, and the course content consists of a workbook of 150–300 pages, written assignments, and a workshop (tutorial) of 2–4 hours with the module tutor. .Other benefits include fulltime contact with a tutor, available via e-mail, and continual updates of Modules on an annual basis. Though unusual in work based learning, there is a two hour written examination required for most modules to assess the students' knowledge based on the particular area*. This examination constitutes 70% of the credit value of the module, and includes both short questions and long essay style questions requiring candidates to demonstrate both basic knowledge and understanding of the material. The assignments require a detailed 3000 word essay describing how the candidate would deal with real world problems in an industrial setting. Employers are keen to assess the performance of employees under a degree of stress, with complete absence of outside help. The skill of self reliance is still highly regarded, in addition to the ability of team work. Although there are other forms of WBL academic achievements discussed in Boud & Solomon (2001), the diet of workbooks, workshops and formative assessments in conjunction with summative assessment in the form of assignments and exams is highly regarded by industrial partners, and the majority of uptake of new modules and awards is repeat business from satisfied partners. Students can enrol for single modules, or any multiple of their choice. Eight modules should be completed in 4 years, with a final year for the dissertation for the award of MSc.

University Awards and Accreditation

University awards include Module credits, 15 per module, a Diploma for 8x15 credits, and an MSc is gained after the Diploma, plus Dissertation of 60 credits, making a total of 180 credits. In addition to the original programme we have established four new programmes, Clinical Trials, Toxicology, Pharmaceutical Microbiology, and Pharmaceutical Business and Development, each having at least eight modules from which to choose. These additional modules can be used to study for awards in the four specific areas, or alternatively modules from any of the programmes can be selected, dependent on student or employer requirements.

---

*   Examinations are an unusual form of assessment in work based learning, but can reflect the preferences of institutions, fields of study or the employer. Projects, reports, practical applications/observations, presentations and dialogue assessments are more common.

Figure 11.1: PIAT Programmes and Modules

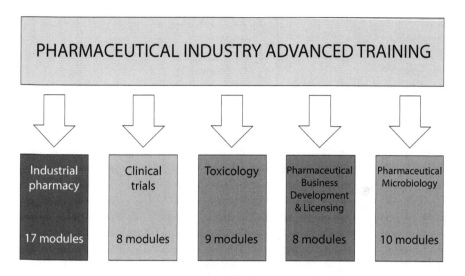

Figure 11.2: PIAT Academic Awards and possible progression

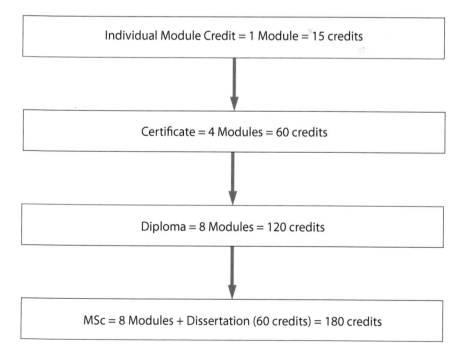

The degree awarded is an Industrial Pharmaceutical Sciences MSc for the original PIAT programme, and the new programmes have an MSc in their specified subject. Five or more modules in one of the four new programmes allow the award in that specialist area. Distinctions are awarded for marks of <70% in all the Modules and the Dissertation, and 12 have been awarded over the last 4 years.

Distance learning at a HEI is equally attractive to employers and employees as well as the HEI. Rigorous quality assurance of both the course and academic content is carried out by the University of Manchester* according to standard processes, which includes:

- A Programme Specification outlining the range of Awards available

- Aims of the programme

- Programme Learning Outcomes in the standard groups of Knowledge and Understanding, Intellectual Skills, Practical Skills and Transferable and Personal Skills

- The programme structure, including curriculum mapping against learning outcomes

- Arrangements for student support and development

All module tutors from academia and industry are accredited University staff, and results are moderated by an accredited external examiner. Unit evaluation forms are completed by all students in order to check for quality service and hopefully elicit new ideas. The progress of the programmes are monitored annually and a major evaluation is carried out every 5 years, involving academic staff from other Schools and Faculties, and is chaired by an outside expert with knowledge of both academia and Pharma.

Funding and Price

As discussed earlier, funding was initially supplied by the four major industrial concerns. After paying for authors to write the modules, the programme became self funding in a stepwise growth. Two new programmes planned in 2007 were funded by Higher Education Funding Council for England (HEFCE) & North West Regional Development Authority (NWRDA), and others by the University of Manchester, or via collaboration. We have two major collaborators,

---

*   Universities also adopt streamlined processes for responsive provision, specifically for accrediting training provision. Timing depends on the provision being accredited, but for example, 6 weeks is a reasonable expectation for short awards of 30–60 credits at level 4.

The Pharmaceutical Microbiology Advanced Training (PMAT) programme was planned in collaboration with Pharmig, a non-profit organisation with a profile of Manufacturing, R&D, Allied Commercial, NHS & Contract labs and was established in 1991 to meet the needs of Pharmaceutical Microbiologists. The Pharmaceutical Business Development and Licensing programme was established in collaboration with UK PLG (The Pharmaceutical Licensing Group). PLG is the professional association for business development and licensing in the industry, and again it is a not for profit organisation, and industry based. The primary role of PLG is networking and continuous professional development.

In the planning stages, the fee structures were considered and compared with comparable MSc courses at other HE institutions. The figure of £12,825 is currently the price for a 180 credit MSc, and although this figure is higher than the cost at many other institutions supplying full time programmes, it is very realistic when the living costs of attending full time programmes are added. The vast majority of the fees are paid by employers, who are making a positive contribution to the student's career.

This collaboration between the three parties worked well; the practical work for the MSc dissertation is carried out at the industrial site, supervised by both academic and industrial supervisors. This instils a research ethos in the student, which is invaluable to both employer and employees for carrying out clearly defined studies with clear outcomes, but with an investigative approach.

Learning Environment

In the PIAT context work based learning is the physical presence of the student on site in the industry, carrying out duties related to manufacture or development of medicines. Employers pay the course fees and give variable time to students for learning or attendance at workshops/examinations. There is a clear impact on the students who are work based learners. They have to learn to balance their time and effort between their employer and themselves. This usually involves evening and/or holiday working to account for the necessary time required for completion of their PIAT qualification, but also allows students to continue in paid employment and live a family life at their site of work. This extra pressure and time planning is excellent training for career progression afterwards.

Financial benefits accrue to both students and employers in terms of time and money spent, the student does not need to leave the workplace and the employer keeps and retains staff during the programme. Other benefits include improved work performance, as evidence by their ability to work independently and take full control of projects and an additional benefit includes career development. One extreme example is that of one student who developed to become a Module tutor.

Impact on staff career progression is a major benefit for stability in the workplace, plus the additional desire of staff to question processes, procedures and intended outcomes of all activities. Simply, this increases competence of individuals and the organisation.

Intended outcomes are well described by students and employers as improved work performance and job satisfaction. Unintended outcomes relate to staff turnover within Pharma, and this is still an issue, and not necessarily a negative influence. Previously employers may have lost staff as part of their business plans, and as well as by unexpected departure. New employers have to attract staff with higher salaries for higher qualifications and these new employees often enforce their experience of PIAT distance learning on new staff to again facilitate training. This dynamic situation, brings benefits to all three parties. The consequences of interaction between students and tutors were not fully predicted, but again it has resulted in a two way dialogue, beyond the confines of the PIAT programmes. Tutors are usually exhilarated by student input during workshops and vice versa. This contact between the parties may develop further as employees network with tutors in the course of their employment as many tutors also act as expert consultants and can attract more contacts.

The Future

To date there have been over 200 MSc completions, and 3000 individual modules gained in the PIAT programmes. Students have come from a wide range of employers including major Pharma, biotech companies and the NHS, and have been mainly staff from Production, and R & D. Worldwide take-up of the programmes includes S. America, N. America, the Far East and Europe. The whole process has taken 21 years since original inception. PIAT programmes are unique to the manufacturing science aspect of the Pharmaceutical industry, in their distance learning format, and have contributed to industry success for nearly 20 years. Although the distance learning format has been widely used in business schools and other industries, PIAT is currently the only institution to employ it in the area of pharmaceutical industrial training. Extended promotion of the programme includes visits to major Pharma, and further presentations at learned conferences, in addition to our exhibitions at British Pharmaceutical Conference (BPC) 2008 and 2009, and European Federation for Pharmaceutical Sciences (EUFEPS) 2009, and e-Newsletter shots to all known HR managers and former students. Recently we have started to explain the benefits of PIAT to industry via articles in pharmaceutical journals such as

EIPG (European Industrial Pharmacy Group) journal and The European Pharmaceutical Review, and have advertised in journals.

Current plans for expansion into further geographical areas include collaboration with KLEC, a Malaysian education specialist, in combination with the major established School of Pharmacy in Malaysia. We plan to mirror our tutor base with specialist staff from this school, and continue our success in the rapidly developing Pharma and biotech industries in the country. Plans for China are also being investigated in an attempt to establish a presence in the largest global market.

In addition to promoting the PIAT programmes overseas, a set of new modules are being developed. We currently have a range of smaller, 1–3 credit unit sized packages in preparation, specifically designed for continual professional development (CPD). It is thought that these will be ideal for CPD, which is increasingly important to both employers and employees in the pharmaceutical industry.

Key Learning Points

1. Industrial employees (students) realise their academic potential while still fully employed at their industrial site

2. Employers retain their services at the same time as employees are further developing their careers

3. All the academic tutors have "hands on" industry experience. Students develop contacts with these international experts (tutors) in their own particular areas of specialisation in which they either currently work or have future plans to do so

4. This collaboration between Pharma industry and the HEI (University of Manchester) has been evolving over 20 years, and available course material has expanded from eight to fifty two modules, encompassing most scientific aspects of pharmaceutical manufacturing. The expanded coverage has been implemented after detailed discussions with acclaimed industry experts

Reference

Boud, D. and Solomon, N. (2001) *Work-based Learning: A New Higher Education.* Buckingham, UK: Open University.

CHAPTER 12

Professionalising the Events Industry. A Work Based Solution for Showsec International

Conor Moss, Head of Learning Solutions, University of Derby Corporate

Keith Hackett, Academy Manager, Showsec International Ltd

Executive Summary

Showsec International Ltd provides security and crowd management at a wide variety of venues, festivals and other events in the UK. The company recognised that in an increasingly complex and competitive industry, where Health and Safety of the public is a major concern, there was a need to develop an education strategy within the management teams of the company, to promote the concepts of professionalism and personal and professional development. However, it was of paramount importance that any education programme was founded in the workplace, drawing on the company's own extensive experiences in events and crowd safety issues, and offered an equal opportunity for those who were new to the industry, as well as those with significant experience, to gain Higher Education qualifications.

This chapter will:

- Outline the Showsec and University of Derby Corporate (UDC) partnership

- Provide a rationale for the main drivers for Showsec in seeking an academic partner

- Discuss the validated Foundation Degree programme and the implementation of the programme

- Provide an opportunity to hear the learner voice and their experiences of the programme

- Highlight some recommendations and conclusions for successful partnership development

Overview of UDC/Showsec

Showsec International Ltd is Europe's leading specialist crowd management and event Security Company providing security and crowd management at a wide variety of venues, festivals and other events in the UK. The company has 90 full-time employees, over 2500 part-time employees and operates in over 450 venues throughout the UK. The Company delivers event security and crowd management services to sport, music, venues, local authorities and artists. Over 30 million people per annum attend public events at which the Company provides Security and Safety services. Showsec has achieved a record score under the Government's Approved Contractors Scheme, which measures the credibility and standards underpinning service delivery within the industry. In addition they have won five consecutive Event Security Team of the Year Awards and for six of the past seven years has been voted the favourite Security and Crowd Management Company by peers within the industry. Showsec also has Investors in People accreditation.

Whilst Showsec strives for commercial success its business is delivered in an ethical manner with strong values. Showsec objectives include *improving and developing industry standards, improving public safety, providing personal opportunity* and *development and acquiring industry and public recognition.*

UDC is the training and development division of the University of Derby. UDC work with a wide variety of organisations to deliver Work Based Learning programmes that improve key capabilities such as service, innovation, leadership and problem solving. Using our academic rigour and commercial experience, we deliver relevant and robust solutions that enable our clients to achieve business benefit through developing their people.

Drivers for Change in the Events Industry

The company recognised that in an increasingly complex and competitive industry, where Health and Safety of the public is a major concern, there was a need to develop an education strategy within the management teams of the company, to promote the concepts of professionalism and personal and professional development.

Bromley and Moss (2009, p.44) outline the complexity of the events industry and the need for professionalisation:

'On the one hand events must push the artistic boundaries of creativity and innovation to deliver consumer experiences (Pine and Gilmore, 1999; Allen et al, 2008) to meet the demands of an increasingly hedonistic society. On the other, organisers must create safe systems of work to comply with their statutory duty, retain reputation and gain repeat custom in an increasingly competitive and litigious business environment (Eve, 2007)'.

Winning a significant contract triggered cultural change within Showsec and a desire to create a fully supported career path. Strategic and business planning resulted in Showsec commissioning a brand new work based qualification.

It was against this background that Showsec first approached five Universities in the autumn of 2009 to source a partner that could coherently structure their Academy Programme at HE Level. There was a competitive 'pitch' process and as a result of several meetings the University of Derby Corporate won the contract in December 2010 to develop and deliver a Foundation Degree in Applied Professional Studies (Crowd Operations Management). The programme was due to start in mid-February 2011 so agility was paramount in terms of validation and development of the programme.

The aims of the programme for Showsec are to:

1. Provide the company with individually competent operational personnel, through a rolling programme of selection and achievement

2. Provide the required numbers of competent personnel to fill positions created by the ongoing company expansion

3. Provide a path for operational development

4. Create opportunity and career paths for staff, as specified in the Business Plan

5. Regularly review and report on the quality of processes employed in the department and customer feedback and ongoing requirements

Flexible and Innovative Programme Design

Central to the programme was its workplace focus, drawing on the company's own extensive experiences in events and crowd safety issues, and offering an equal opportunity for those who were new to the industry, as well as those with significant experience, to gain Higher Education qualifications.

Knowles' (1990) work on adult learning principles was considered in the design and development of the programme. Specifically we considered how *'Adults pursue learning that can be applied immediately'*. In general, adults seek education when there is a problem that requires solving, and specifically for Events Management, this may be upskilling due to a promotion or similar, changes to legislation or bringing qualifications up to date. The course therefore had to be compact, with flexible assessments that impact on the work that the learner is involved with.

As we developed the programme it was apparent that the need for numerous step-in and step-off points for the learner was of paramount importance. Consequently we developed 5 smaller awards within the Foundation Degree. Figure 12.1 below shows how a range of shorter award outcomes is available within the two stages of the overarching FdA programme.

Figure 12.1: Overview of the FdA Applied Professional Studies (Crowd Management)

Year 1 – FdA Applied Professional Studies (Crowd Management)

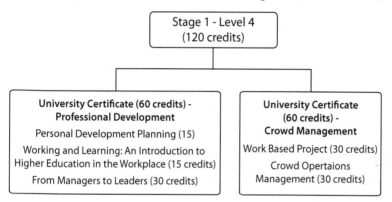

* Both of these modules have also been developed as Certificate of Achievement programme for a broader audience within Showsec and for the industry in general

Year 2 – FdA Applied Professional Studies (Crowd Management)

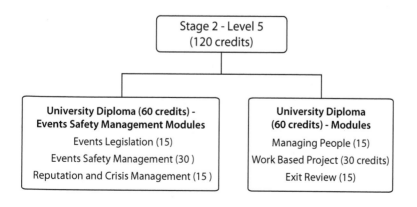

UDC and Showsec – The first year

We have enrolled over 50 people on different awards. The minimum credit achievement has been 45 credits. Twelve learners completed the Level 5 Events Safety Diploma in time to apply their higher level learning at work during the busy 2011 outdoor festival season.

From the beginning, a key element of the programme, embedded at all levels, has been reflective practice and the capturing of that reflection. As the programme has developed, the value of its Reflective Portfolio in supporting learners' emerging perceptions of themselves as leaders and learners has been continually reinforced. The following extracts, taken from entries made during and after the 'leadership week', a residential course, held in Derbyshire for each group of learners, demonstrates this clearly.

Excerpts from the 'Leadership Week'

'By the end of the week we had managed to move through all the development stages without even realising it. In work, the staff are still probably at the forming stage because there is very little opportunity for them to go beyond that at the moment. When they come to work on a festival site, they may move through the stages given the right direction. As for the operations team, we have probably moved through all the stages on a regular basis. This, ideally, needs to be transferred right down to the casual staff. However, it is much easier for the operations team because we work together on a much more regular basis, where as the casual staff work with each other not so often'.

The concept of learning and reflective practice was introduced in the Induction session, together with a presentation of Kolb's Learning Cycle Model (1984). Learning activities were organized broadly in line with Kolb's thinking. This meant that learners would have an experience, reflect on that experience, draw conclusions from it and then try out what they had learned.

Learners were supported throughout by an online portal customised specifically for the company and its learning programmes. The portal's facility for building an e-Portfolio and keeping continuous reflective learning records ensured that this process was seamless and embedded to everyday practice.

The following figure shows a live page from the portal, with the learner's reflection and the tutor's formative feedback.

Figure 12.2: Example of a Reflective Learning Record

Entry Title:	Review of Leading teams questionnaire
Entry Date:	24/03/2011

Reflection on course content:

My review on my results was as follows. All my scores were within the moderate range, I have always through different employment lead teams and in some cases these have been in dangerous situations. My lowest score was within the Fostering team spirit. The first area is to solve problems collectively as part of a team, this area again I need to gain trust in my teams ability. I know that the teams I work with have a lot of knowledge but I need to gain trust and accept that a group of ideas may be better than just mine. Also to adapt my team members I need them to want to contribute, I am going to work on standing back and letting others suggest idea and accept that there ideas could work better than mine. With regards to a team having fun, I believe that I may have under graded this area as my venues have a good relationship between them, I just make sure it stays professional and that nobody will be offended by what is being said. Fun is good and I always promote this but there is sometimes a time a place, I am going to see if I can see when banter is the right time.

Personal Statements of Learning:

Again looking at the feedback I received I am a strong leader and do like to stand up and give my opinion. I was told that I must try and give other a chance.

Reflect upon your personal and professional application and/or experiences of this learning:

I am going to look at standing back, this I will link closely to the motivating others as they do work closely alongside each other. I am going to hand over tasks to others and stand back to let them run the task with me over seeing how they complete it. I may set the task some targets which have to be achieved.

Outline steps for Continuing Personal and Professional Development:

ASSESSOR COMMENTS

Please use the text box below to add your comments:

A very comprehensive overview of your experiences throughout the course of the week and specifically your areas for personal and professional development. You clearly are highly motivated to succeed and this can be attested by you willingness Ito lead from the front.

Conor

A Developing Partnership

The relationship between Showsec and UDC continues apace with more enrolments than first expected onto the Foundation Degree and new areas of joint work. For example, we have developed a bespoke Training and Development Portal for all of Showsec's Operational training needs and continue to explore broader commercial relationships for the national and international market. Originally, UDC delivered all components of the programme, however Showsec have now been confirmed as Accredited Partners of the University to deliver the Crowd Operations Management and Work Based Project module. This process has involved the Showsec training team completing the University of Derby's Supporting Work Based Learning programme (Level 7, 30 credits). In Figure 12.3 we have included an overview of our end-to-end Learning and Development work with Showsec across the various vocational and academic levels.

Figure 12.3: Diagram illustrating the various qualifications and intended audience

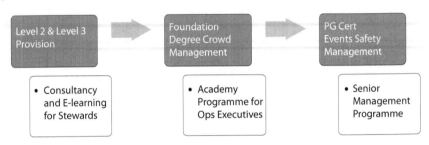

Figure 12.4: E-learning platform that enables all levels of personnel within the organisation to access training and development

Learner Viewpoint

As this is a work based learning programme it is important to hear the learner voice, below are excerpts from the feedback we received about the delegate's experiences on the University programme.

What Attracted You to the Showsec Academy Programme?

'I had been working with Showsec for many years and I had aspired to progress through the company, and the Showsec academy gave me the perfect opportunity to do that. I was able to move to London to do the programme. I was certainly attracted to the challenge, stepping out of my comfort zone and learning what I had always wanted to learn. I was attracted to being able to work along side some of the existing operations executives and area managers to learn from them too.'

How Did The Academy Programme Help Your Personal and Professional Development?

'On a professional level, I have certainly developed with my new operational knowledge, I am able to put the theory we have studied into practice.. The knowledge we have been given is a base for us to build on and every event I work I feel like I build on the knowledge.. The academy has helped me become more flexible in my management styles, and learn how to adapt to other peoples styles.

The Academy has taught me to stop rushing into things, the Academy has given me the knowledge to work with, and I needed to stop rushing into things. I can do that now; I can step back from the situations and make informed decisions. This is something I have applied personally in my life. Also I think I have matured both at work and in personally, in how I look at, and judge certain situations.'

Recommendations and Conclusions

University Viewpoint

Recommendations for winning new business, delivering an excellent service and building relationships

1. When pitching to employers the solution has to be clearly defined, transparent in pricing and flexible to allow for the changing business environment

2. Innovation and creativity is vital to ensure Work Based Learning principles are embedded throughout the programme therefore driving real business change

3. Assessment needs to be fit for purpose, work related and appropriate for professional and academic purposes

4. Whilst there is a need to validate a programme of study prior to delivery it is essential that the Learning, Teaching and Assessment strategy is continually reviewed to ensure it evolves in line with the organisations' business needs

5. The management of internal expectations in relation to income, workloads of academic staff and willingness to travel is vital to ensure that your best people are 'enabled' to deliver an excellent service.

6. Universities have much to offer employers and any corporate partnership should be a window to the various areas of expertise and not limited to one subject area.

Employer Viewpoint

Recommendations for selecting and working with a University partner

1. Take the time to properly scope your business requirements so that you can clearly articulate your needs to a third party

2. Offer a range of providers the opportunity to pitch for the business through a formal tender process or a series of proposals that enable you to select the correct University partner

3. Ask questions of the partner that tests their flexibility, innovation and ability to think differently

4. Ensure that all aspects of the programme are as transparent as possible to enable open and frank discussions

5. Build Return on Investment (ROI) measurement and evaluation into the programme from the outset to enable you to justify the Learning and Development spend

6. Make full use of the University support systems in terms of access to learning resources, CPD activities and breadth of knowledge e.g. we have worked with University of Derby Corporate to develop a bespoke Learning Platform

7. Ensure you have a rapport with the development and delivery team so that feedback the relationship can be evolutionary

8. Plan, do and review! Our programme is changing with each cohort that we run to ensure the content stays current and delivers on our business needs

In conclusion, this chapter demonstrates a journey taken by three parties with different work pressures that must work flexibly together to ensure success, often against competing work and programme pressures. The key to continued success is in reviewing the Learning, Teaching and Assessment strategy to ensure it evolves in line with the organisations' business needs. The combined industry experience of Showsec and educational expertise of University of Derby Corporate has enabled the company to introduce new leadership skills to develop a fully rounded operational experience ultimately resulting in a safer environment for all those attending public and commercial entertainment events.

It has been a unique and groundbreaking achievement within the security industry. Showsec has completed this stage of its programme and has witnessed ongoing commercial expansion since 2007, undoubtedly related to the quality of its management development programme. At the time of writing Showsec had been shortlisted for the National Training Awards for the above programme.

References

Allen, J., O'Toole W., Harris, R., McDonnell I. 2008. Festival & special event management, 4th ed. Milton, QLD.4064, John Wiley & Sons Australia, Ltd

Eve, A. (2007) of project management systems, Industrial and Commercial Training. (2) . 85–90.

Knowles, M. (1990) The Adult Learner: A Neglected Species, 4th edition (Houston, Gulf Publishing Company).

Kolb, D. A. (1984) Experiential Learning, Englewood Cliffs, NJ. Prentice Hall

Moss, C & Bromley, M (2009) Towards a 'community of practice' for events safety. Work Based Learning Futures III, Bolton, University Awards Vocational Council

Pine, B., J. and Gilmore, J., H. (1999) Experience Economy, The Work Is Theatre and Every Business a Stage, Harvard business press.

CHAPTER 13

Best of Both? Adding Value to Work-related Learning through a University-Private Training Provider Partnership

Celia Moran, Director Escalate Programme, University of Bradford

Executive Summary

Established in 1995, Winning Moves is a business improvement consultancy that aims to make a measurable and sustainable difference to business, people and places with an offer that includes a suite of performance improvement tools for business, support organisations and advisers; and a wide range of consultancy and training programmes for both independent businesses and the public and voluntary sectors.

Winning Managers is a year-long leadership and management training programme which had originally been developed and delivered by Winning Moves as a standalone programme. It was subsequently incorporated as part of a larger business development intervention often delivered via public sector regeneration or enterprise initiatives. The programme had been delivered for a range of corporate clients including KPMG, and other private, public and voluntary sector organisations, usually to new and aspiring middle managers in the case of larger organisations but also to owner-managers of Small and Medium Enterprises (SMEs).

Winning Moves were seeking to add further value to this training through University accreditation and engaged in an EBTA type process to identify a suitable partner through West Yorkshire Lifelong Learning Network (WYLLN). This process gave rise to University of Bradford being identified as the preferred partner, and led to the accreditation of Winning Managers as a Certificate of Higher Education.

Winning Moves have been approved as a collaborative partner by University of Bradford and the Winning Managers programme has received academic approval. It is now ready to be launched and delivered by Winning Moves.

This case study explores the underlining rationale and principles associated with the partnership, explains the roles of the various stakeholders, describes the partnership journey, and discusses the opportunities it might afford, the issues arising, and lessons learned.

The case study highlights the following:

- The value of business-provider networks such as Lifelong Learning Networks and **fdf** in brokering relationships

- The value of a flexible 'shell' framework in facilitating the accreditation of training

- The important role of academic staff in 'translating' training into an academic programme and in contributing to the design of assessment

- The need for understanding and 'buy in' by colleagues across the University, not just those directly involved in employer engagement

- The volatility and risk associated with 'business-facing' activity

Developing the Partnership between Winning Moves and University of Bradford

The relationship between Winning Moves and University of Bradford was brokered by a project funded and managed by the (WYLLN). One of 30 Lifelong Learning Networks (LLNs) across England, the WYLLN is a partnership of higher education institutions, further education colleges, training providers and sector skills councils throughout West Yorkshire (West Yorkshire Lifelong Learning Network 2007). WYLLN had developed and funded a higher level skills coordinator role in each of five local authority areas. The role of these coordinators was to raise the profile of higher level skills among employers, help businesses understand the HE 'offer' and support and influence local employment and skills boards (see Chapter 15). As part of this activity WYLLN had also worked with the EBTA team to provide staff development and raise capacity for the delivery of an EBTA type service in West Yorkshire.

The Leeds Higher Level Skills Coordinator was based with Leeds, York and North Yorkshire Chamber and it was through the Chamber that Winning Moves became aware of the EBTA service and the opportunities afforded by the accreditation of their training package. Winning Moves were working with Leeds, York and North Yorkshire Chamber in the delivery of organisational change and leadership programmes: an offer which included their 'Winning Managers' programme. The Winning Moves approach integrates organisational and individual development and in relation to the latter, they identified the benefits and potential market for accredited training that contributes to an individual's continuing professional development, gives reward and recognition for learning achievement and the opportunity to progress with credit or advanced standing to a University award. What was crucial to them was the combination of a flexible and tailored training package that meets the requirements of their client organisations, with the added value of university accreditation. The first phase of the partnership development was therefore modelled upon the EBTA 'expression of interest' process whereby in this case the Leeds Higher Level Skills Co-ordinator undertook the evaluation of Winning Moves' Winning Managers programme and issued an invitation for expressions of interest among the West Yorkshire HE providers. This process, and the meetings that followed, resulted in University of Bradford being selected as the preferred partner to undertake the accreditation.

At the highest level, the University of Bradford strategic impetus to engage with this accreditation opportunity came through its long standing objectives in relation to 'Making Knowledge Work' and a corporate strategy which states that:

'Our priorities will be about flexible provision, continuing professional development, providing graduates with premium skills, addressing the higher skills needs of today's and tomorrow's workforce.' (University of Bradford, 2009).

Escalate, a University of Bradford employer engagement programme funded by the Higher Education Funding Council for England (HEFCE) has, between 2008 and 2011, been pivotal to the delivery of that University strategy. Escalate was charged with developing and embedding , through demonstrator projects, a more flexible and responsive academic infrastructure, more suited to meeting the needs of employers and employee learners, addressing matters of costing and pricing and student administration, as well as academic course approval and collaborative provision processes. The Escalate Programme had a number of key outputs in its business plan, including the accreditation of in-company training programmes and the recruitment of HEFCE co-funded employer engagement (CFEE) Additional Student Numbers (ASNs), which the Winning Moves collaboration was to contribute to.

In responding to the Expression of Interest invitation, the Escalate team worked with the School of Lifelong Education and Development who would ultimately become responsible for managing the relationship with Winning Moves and assuring the quality and standards of the programme on behalf of the University. The School of

Lifelong Education and Development offers 'higher education for all' (University of Bradford, 2011), and prides itself in its flexible, work related, community and partner college learning. The Winning Moves proposition provided an opportunity for the School of Lifelong Education and Development to build on its experience in this area, develop an innovative and flexible product, and reach new and complementary employer and student markets. The new programme would become part of a suite of vocational management courses, building upon and complementing existing foundation degree provision, including the Foundation Degree in Leadership and Management, and potentially providing an additional progression route into the School's MA Professional Studies. Of all the academic schools at the University of Bradford, Lifelong Education and Development probably has the most experience of developing and delivering higher level skills programmes that meet the requirements of employers and employee learners and they have become the school that has worked most closely with Escalate in developing accreditation activities.

Partnership and Curriculum Development

Like most other awarding HEIs, the Bradford quality assurance procedure for a programme delivered by a partner has two distinct elements, academic approval and partner approval. The underlying principle being, that an award made following a programme delivered by a partner should be of the same academic standard as other equivalent awards of the University, and that students should have comparable opportunities to reach that standard. Therefore, in order to achieve these necessary approvals the work moved to a much more detailed phase between academic staff in the School of Lifelong Education and Development and the Winning Moves staff who would deliver the programme.

Having agreed with the initial evaluation, that the Winning Managers programme had the potential to be developed into an accredited programme of 120 credits at level 6, the plan was to seek approval for a Certificate of Higher Education in Professional Studies under the University's Undergraduate Professional Studies Shell Framework. This 'shell' framework is an overarching award infrastructure and academic approval process for work based learning, aligned with the Framework for Higher Education Qualifications (FHEQ, August 2008), through which customised programmes of study can be designed, negotiated and approved. The shell framework is expressed in generic terms, with a relatively high degree of optionality. There is flexibility in content and learning approaches and what is important is that learners are able to demonstrate the attainment of module, level and award learning outcomes and that their learning experience provides the opportunity for them to do this.

Figure 13.1: Winning Managers and Professional Studies Shell Framework

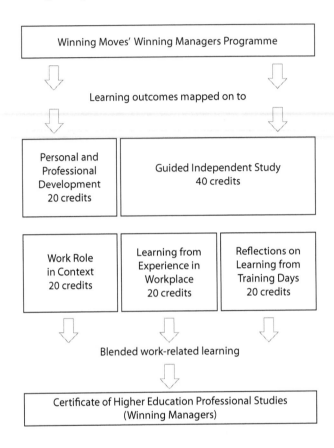

The shell framework has associated with it an academic approval process which, compared to traditional University processes, is streamlined according to risk. This allows for Chair's Action or sub-committee approval for lower level or shorter awards, resulting in a more rapid turn-around than is usually the case. This combination of flexible curricula and a more responsive approval process makes the shell framework particularly suitable for employer-responsive provision and accreditation of in-company training.

During this curriculum development phase discussions and deliberations centred on:

- Mapping the Winning Managers programme to the learning outcomes and modules of the University of Bradford Professional Studies 'shell' framework

- Designing appropriate assessments that satisfied the Professional Studies framework and were suitable for learners in their employment context

- Considering learning resources and how they would be accessed. Winning Moves have their own Virtual Learning Environment (VLE) through which learners access course materials, learning resources and tutor/peer support. This has been developed into a single gateway which interfaces with, and allows access to the University website and VLE

- Supporting and developing Winning Moves' staff in relation to academic expectations

- Clarifying the arrangements for management, quality assurance, resources, support, communication etc, that are required for the approval of collaborative provision

- Agreeing the initial costing and pricing of the programme and producing a business plan that demonstrated financial sustainability

With input and support by Winning Moves staff, the outcome of this phase of the process was the various items of documentation required for formal University approval, with full approval and accreditation achieved early in 2011. While the approval process progressed relatively smoothly, this programme was one of the first to follow the shell framework procedures and so both the concept and the process was new to the course approval panel and there was some lack of clarity about exactly what information and level of detail were required. For the University, the accreditation of Winning Managers served as a useful 'pilot' for the shell framework and identified areas of staff development and guidance that needed to be developed for both approval panel members and programme teams, so that all parties are fully appraised of the documentation requirements and their roles and responsibilities.

At the time of writing, this programme has been accredited by the University of Bradford, but not yet delivered. Along with other employer engagement initiatives, progress is now being hampered by the changed economic context and particularly the impact of public expenditure cuts on the public and voluntary sectors. However, Winning Moves are confident in the product we have developed together. Marketing material has been produced, again in collaboration, using Winning Moves' designers and University printing resources, and the programme is being actively promoted through established networks, with a view to delivering to a first cohort from September 2011.

Opportunities, Learning and Outstanding Issues

For the University, this arrangement is effectively a pilot programme both for the use of its 'shell' award framework, for the accreditation of 'in-company' training and for the approval of a private training provider as a collaborative partner. The experience of establishing the relationship is already feeding into a review of policies and procedures for future academic partnerships and there will be further reflection and evaluation as the relationship continues to unfold. For Winning Moves it has been an opportunity to develop and trial a new product at minimal cost and with the support of experienced facilitators such as EBTA and WYLLN. Both parties benefitted considerably, not only from the opportunity afforded by EBTA initiative, but by the way in which those working within the various complementary employer engagement initiatives (EBTA, WYLLN, Escalate) were able to broker the relationship through sets of complementary and overlapping networks.

The detailed curriculum mapping work undertaken by the academic staff and the training providers was a positive experience for those involved, enhancing understanding and deepening the relationship, as well as producing the documentation and evidence required for academic approval.

The approval process took around six months, much longer than would be ideal for employer-responsive provision, and had we been able to get to market sooner we may have been able to establish the programme before the present 'cut backs' began to bite. However the opportunity to pilot the shell framework has enabled 'sticking points' and bottle-necks to be identified. The costing and pricing methodology and the form of contract for example, are both new. The templates are now in place for similar future development. A lesson reiterated, rather than learned, is perhaps the importance of the relationship between the individuals concerned. All parties have found the others to be open, honest, communicative and understanding, and in general very professional and easy to work with. In this way, barriers and issues have been discussed and addressed along the way in an open and timely fashion. To date everyone has done all they could to make the partnership work.

The main issue now facing the partnership is that of the external economic context. This has seriously impacted upon the intended and potential market for the programme, initially among SMEs and more recently among the public and voluntary sectors. This is now further exacerbated by the reductions in HEFCE income and the pending new fee regime, which will inevitably result in higher prices for this type of provision.

Lessons Learned

- The funding and support provided by the Higher Education Funding Council for England Workforce Development Programme (HEFCE) has been enormously beneficial in providing an infrastructure to facilitate business-university collaborations. This fund has facilitated organisations and networks like WYLLN, *fdf*/EBTA and Escalate which have enable opportunities such as this to be developed

- A flexible shell award framework can be very useful in enabling a University to work responsively with a training provider or employer, both in terms of the curriculum and the approval process

- It is important to have streamlined systems, processes and templates in place, which are clear and well understood, in order to respond in a timely fashion

- Collaborative provision in particular involves a wide range of University services who all need to be willing to work responsively to meet external requirements

- Working with businesses exposes Universities to the volatility of the market and the current climate reinforces the need to be aware of potential risks and to be responsive to changing markets and contexts

References

HEFCE, http://www.hefce.ac.uk/econsoc/employer/ accessed 10/06/11

QAA (Aug 2008) The framework for higher education qualifications in England, Wales and Northern Ireland, August 2008 (FHEQ). Available at http://www.qaa.ac.uk/academicinfrastructure/FHEQ/EWN108/FHEQ08.pdf (accessed 06/05/11)

University of Bradford (2009), Corporate Strategy 2009–14.

University of Bradford (2011) http://www.brad.ac.uk/sled/index.php (accessed 06/05/11)

West Yorkshire Lifelong Learning Network (2007) http://www.wylln.ac.uk/about_us (accessed 10/06/11)

CHAPTER 14

Delivering and Evidencing Business Impact through Higher Level Skills – How the EBTA Process of Accrediting in-house Training Adds Real Business Value

Alix Pearson, Associate Director, **fdf**

Dr Ruth Helyer, Head of Workforce Development, Teesside University

Executive Summary

When investing in a higher level learning programme, employers are looking for change, for transformation of people, products or services. The training is the input and the changes made are the output. How does an employer know what has changed, or by how much, or if the training programme was responsible for it? A systematic process of evaluation can evidence such a chain of impact. This chapter looks at how the process of having an employer's training accredited can make a contribution to providing evaluation evidence of the effectiveness of the programme being accredited. In order for an employer's training to be suitable for academic credit it needs to have intended learning outcomes and proper assessment of those learning outcomes. Such assessment regularly extends beyond an examination of knowledge and understanding to the requirement for a detailed analysis of how the learner has put their knowledge into practice at work. Using Phillip's model of return on investment evaluation, this chapter shows how carefully designed work-based assessment can serve two purposes. Through reporting on the impact of changed actions at work, the trainee has completed a work based assignment. This gets academic credit for the student and provides a valuable implementation report for the employer.

Work Based Learning and its Accreditation

Higher Education (HE) level study is designed to be an exciting, but challenging and stretching experience. When this HE study is based upon a student's workplace/ sector and their work expertise, it becomes more personally appropriate and relevant to needs, but at the same time, more complex. Over the last 10 years, alongside the rise of Foundation degrees, Higher Education Institutions (HEIs) have developed ways to provide vocationally relevant education on a flexible basis. This includes the accreditation of in-company training which can provide an excellent tool to engage employers in higher education in a way which is responsive and directly addresses their needs.

Accreditation processes have grown from the fact that HE level learning carries credit. This is what makes it possible to offer awards and qualifications, the credit system is in place to track and quantify what is *learned*, and furthermore to compare this learning to other learning which is of a similar level of difficulty and complexity. Credit is used in the HE sector as a tool for describing the comparability of learning achieved in terms of its volume and intellectual demand. Because HE level learning carries credit, study pathways can be developed in ways which are flexible, adaptable, valued, tailor-made and tied into a recognised quality system. The HE credit system recognises successful completion of modules, courses and programmes (Helyer 2010:2).

Demand for accreditation depends on employers valuing academic credit. If companies think that their training programmes are robust and provide the knowledge and skills their employees need to meet or improve their workplace performance, then they may not see that HE level credit can bring any added value. This is particularly the case when the accreditation of an in-company programme requires additional work from the employer, such as adding a clearly defined assessment method.

For work-based learners the learning process takes place in the workplace and/or the classroom, further enhanced and facilitated and supported by electronic and mobile technologies and often supported by experienced workplace coaches. When the students are already undertaking training and learning which can be seen to be at HE level (mapped against an HEI's level descriptors for example (see Chapter 19) then there is usually a good case for accrediting this learning and even in adding facets which make the learning more bespoke. The accreditation process adds value for the student as well as offering progression opportunities, both at work and onto further HE study routes, hence encouraging the development of a lifelong learning mentality. An employer's internal training programme can, potentially, be transformed into a format which can carry a realistic amount of academic credit, by combining carefully selected work-based learning with academic input and assessment. Accrediting work-based learning (what is learned at, through and for work) illustrates for employers the higher levels at which their staff are operating and engaging with HE innovations. It allows for a comparison against other programmes using level descriptors and module and programme outlines. Accreditation of company work-based learning also requires that the employed learners actively reflect on their learning process, this can create a powerful synergy between what is learned and how that learning is harnessed and utilised.

Accreditation from an HEI can bring an enhanced status to in-house training as well as putting a useful frame around ongoing staff development This is crucial for employees who may have to change jobs and roles several times in their career. In the current global market anything that helps employees to articulate what they can do and what they know can only enhance their chances of success in an increasingly competitive market where transferable life skills are crucial.

For work-based learners' study to 'count' as HE level they need to demonstrate the development of intellectual, personal, critical and analytical skills, which will support and complement their practical skills and knowledge. The *fdf* Employer-based Training Accreditation (EBTA) process offers an established way for these key attributes to be brought together in a powerful collaboration.

When employers invest in training and education for their staff it seems obvious, and fair, that they would be looking for some kind of return on that investment (ROI). The ideal scenario would be to see a marked increase in the productivity and profitability of the business and to be able to track this increase back to the effects of the training interventions. However, it is notoriously difficult to prove and quantify to what exactly such improvements are directly attributable, because many factors influence the bottom line. Those undertaking the actual studying, the employees, often have differing and more finite motives such as: learning/knowing more; discovering how to use and enhance what they know; fulfilling their potential; increasing earnings; getting/keeping job; gaining promotion and so on. To the student, accreditation has a tangible value as academic credits are transportable to other job roles and other employers, they offer progression and can be 'cashed in' towards other qualifications.

EBTA and ROI

If the employer is to appreciate equally the power of academic credit then accredited training needs to be carefully planned and assessed. The ROI theory described below offers a useful way to approach this with the potential to map the assessment strategy against a tried and tested ROI model. In the current economic climate, many training managers are being asked to justify or demonstrate the ROI for education and training projects. The use of Quality management methodologies have provided management with information about efficiency and productivity, by initiating improvement projects which follow a defined sequence of steps and have quantified financial targets. This interest in measurement, evaluation and accountability has travelled to some Human Resources departments who are being asked to measure their contribution to business success and profitability. To *think* that training adds value and makes a difference is one thing, to be able to articulate and demonstrate the difference it *actually* makes is another.

Evaluation of courses of learning brings to mind 'happy sheets' These are questionnaires handed out at the end of a training day which enquire whether the participants liked the lunch and enjoyed the programme. A more rigorous evaluation methodology is that of Donald Kirkpatrick, which is widely used as the HR industry standard model of training evaluation. This methodology comprises four escalating levels of evaluation, each of which investigates the impact of the training programme more deeply than the previous level.

Table 14.1: Kirkpatrick's four levels of training evaluation

1	Reaction	Reaction evaluation is how the delegates felt about the training or learning experience
2	Learning	Learning evaluation is the measurement of the increase in knowledge after the programme
3	Application	Application evaluation is the extent to which the learning is applied back on the job
4	Business Impact	Business Impact evaluation measures the effect on the business of the participant's changed behaviour

This model shows that 'happy sheets' are not an irrelevant part of evaluation, they are instead the first part of a planned process of gathering and analysing data about training programmes.

The Phillips ROI methodology builds on the work of Donald Kirkpatrick and his 4 level model of evaluation, and adds value to this by creating a clear connection and alignment with SPECIFIC business needs.

Table 14.2: Phillip's model of Business Needs Alignment

Business Needs Alignment (Phillips)	Evaluation (Kirkpatrick)
Potential Payoff	ROI
Business Needs – solving problems or taking opportunities	Business Impact
Job performance needs – doing something new, or better	Application & performance change
Skill/knowledge needs – what learning is required?	Learning & confidence
Stakeholder preferences – what take-up is right for the business?	Reaction & action planning

It is the focus on the business needs which allows training evaluation to become ROI evaluation. Kirkpatrick's model evaluates the impact of the training, but without the alignment to specific business needs, there is nothing with which to compare the evaluation outcome.

Understanding that you have achieved a ROI in training programmes does not happen by accident. It happens because there has been a considered process of business needs analysis and training solution implementation, all linked to important measures of business performance. If training programmes are selected without any particular business improvement in mind, or if they are selected because the HR manager feels the content is valuable in a general sense, demonstrating any link between business improvement and the training programme, using the Phillips method, will be impossible.

Learning which takes place in the workplace, applied and supported in a workplace setting, can contribute to very high ROI values. A carefully designed programme of HE using work-based learning can make a significant contribution to the evidencing of impact in the workplace. Effective ROI evaluations can be time consuming and require specialist skills and knowledge. However, the principles inherent in Phillips ROI model can be used as a route map for assessment design, ensuring that the assessments necessary for EBTA accreditation also reflect the relevant stages of the ROI model, as shown below.

Table 14.3: A Model of HE accreditation activity as evidence towards training evaluation

Business Needs Alignment Stages (Phillips) to be considered by the Employer		Accredition Acitivities to be undertaken by the University		Evaluation Steps (Kirkpatrick) – can be met jointly by employer and accrediting university
Potential Payoff	↓		→	ROI
Understanding business needs for training – solving problems or taking opportunities	↓	Designing assessments which collect work based evidence of execution of action plans and the outcome of planned projects	→	Business Impact

Business Needs Alignment Stages (Phillips) to be considered by the Employer		Accredition Acitivities to be undertaken by the University		Evaluation Steps (Kirkpatrick) – can be met jointly by employer and accrediting university
What job performance changes are required who needs to do something new, or better	↓	Incorporating personal action planning, creation of learning contracts, personal development plans, portfolios of evidence of changed behaviour, into assessments	→	Application & performance change
What are their skill/ knowledge needs – what learning is required	↓	Delivering underpinning knowledge or relevant principles and theories	→	Learning & confidence
Understanding stakeholder preferences – what take-up is right for the business	→	Ensuring programme accessibility through consultative design	→	Reaction & action planning

EBTA Case Study

A hotel group which owns over 20 luxury hotels in the UK submitted their internal Spa Management programme to EBTA for accreditation. As this was a new business direction for the company, the programme was designed as a response to the new business opportunity at level 4 in the table above. The programme was comprehensive in its content and rigorous in its delivery, but prior to accreditation, had no assessment action. The EBTA consultant started the accreditation process by understanding the business need for the Spa Management programme. The consultant discovered that, whilst the spa was a new business opportunity, there had been early problems relating to profitability and staff satisfaction. Investigation, at business need level 3, (see Table 14.2), 'who needs to do something different or better?' showed that therapists were struggling to keep all the appointments in their schedule, resulting in overrunning, lateness and customer complaints. A more strategic and systematic approach to appointment scheduling was needed. The skills and knowledge requirement (level 2 on Table 14.1) was for operational managers to have a sound understanding of all spa processes, procedures, costs and profitability. Whilst the training programme covered some complex areas of knowledge, borrowing scheduling procedures from the engineering sector, it lacked a compulsion to action plan and apply the learning. The EBTA consultant made some suggestions about what kind of assessment would be appropriate and acceptable for HE accreditation and the training manager designed a project. Programme participants needed to undertake an investigation and a staff consultation to gain as much knowledge as possible about specific problems in their spa area and gather suggestions for improvement. After analysing this information, participants needed to design and implement a new appointment system, drawing up criteria against which they would evaluate its effectiveness. Once the evaluation was showing evidence of improvement against the evaluation criteria, the programme participants needed to train relevant staff to use the system, explaining how and why it operates. Finally, participants completed a report to their hotel manager, illustrating the changes in spa capacity, profitability and customer satisfaction.

These reports provided the hotel group with a large amount of valuable and commercially sensitive information, which demonstrated the direct impact of application of the training course content. The content covered simple information about the nature of every treatment on offer in the spa, coupled with complex information about how to achieve the most profitable return from expensive capital equipment. However, it was the requirement to apply the knowledge and report on its impact, which really added and demonstrated the value of the programme to the company.

Conclusion

Well-constructed workplace training which carries academic credit should offer a 'win-win' situation for the employer and employee. The win for the employer is the potential of having evidence of the impact that the training has made in the workplace which may be demonstrated in work-based projects. The win for the HEI is the opportunity to have a cost effective way of engaging with business. Clearly, the reality of this is complex as agreements need to be made over who pays for what, what time off for study, if any, is to be allowed, and crucially, what happens if a student fails a work-based assessment. The accrediting HEI can offer advice and support in these areas based on many years of experience. The accrediting HEI may find itself with a complex set of relationships to manage with their client, the employer who has requested the accreditation, and also with the client's employees, who become the university's students. Although complex, such partnerships can bring valuable benefits. The withdrawal of public funding for many HE courses means that some course fees will rise up to £9,000 per year from September 2012. The accreditation of in-house training can offer a cost effective way of engaging with HE for both individuals and businesses. Accrediting in-house training offers opportunities for universities to collaborate with employers in the joint development of higher level education which combines the best of knowledge of both parties.

References

Helyer, R., (2010) 'Introduction' in *The Work-Based Learning Student Handbook* (Basingstoke: Palgrave Macmillan).

Kirkpatrick, D. L. and Kirkpatrick, J.D. (2009) *Evaluating Training Programs*, 6th ed., Berrett Koehler, San Francisco.

Phillips, J. J. (2003) *Return on Investment in Training and Performance Improvement Programs*. 2nd ed. Burlington MA: Butterworth-Heinemann. P ix

CHAPTER 15

West Yorkshire Lifelong Learning Network Higher Level Skills Coordinator Roles

Ian McGregor-Brown, Higher Level Skills Coordinator for Employment and Skills, West Yorkshire Lifelong Learning Network

Joanne Beaumont, Assistant Director, West Yorkshire Lifelong Learning Network

Executive Summary

This chapter offers an insight into the establishment of Higher Level Skills Coordinators (HLSC), funded by the West Yorkshire Lifelong Learning Network (WYLLN). The establishment of HLSC was in response to two issues, firstly the messages received from businesses regarding the difficulty encountered in engaging with Higher Education (HE) providers and secondly the wish to engage with and influence regional skills strategies via the Employment & Skills Boards.

Through the work of the HLSC clear messages have been received from businesses in relation to how HE providers need to alter approaches in order to secure business and these are provided together with suggested ways forward. The influence on regional skills strategies is discussed briefly and demonstrates the response of WYLLN partners to the changing skills landscape and the sustainability of methods of partnership securing a voice within key strategic bodies.

Background Context and Positioning

WYLLN was established in 2007 as part of a national programme of Lifelong Learning Networks with funding for three years from the Higher Education Funding Council for England (HEFCE).

The WYLLN's aim was to 'strengthen the performance of West Yorkshire businesses and the regional economy through improved vocational and work-based progression of young people and adults into and through higher education (HE)'. As such, WYLLN's focus from the start and throughout has been on addressing the higher level skills agenda and it has done this by developing curricula, progression routes, services, products and networks which aim to meet the needs of vocational learners and business.

WYLLN had meaningful engagement with over three thousand businesses. The overwhelming message coming out of those interactions was that business does not understand the 'offer', that is what services and products the HE sector already provides, or could provide, which are specifically designed for, and aimed at, the business and/or work-based learner markets for example short courses, accredited and non-accredited, Continuous Professional Development (CPD), professional training, accreditation services and so on.

Alongside this, discussions and partnership working with Business Link at regional, sub-regional and local levels suggested that the knowledge level and breadth of many business link advisers in regard to higher level skills and the HE sector was limited, as echoed by businesses. Analysis of skills needs identified and referral data from Business Link by sub-region and local authority area suggested limited brokerage activity taking place in relation to higher level skills, and in particular referrals to higher education providers.

These two pieces of evidence in particular prompted WYLLN during mid 2009 to reflect on what actions it might take both at a strategic and operational level to address the issues identified by adding value to the existing business engagement activities of partner institutions and stakeholders, whilst taking care to avoid duplication of service and creating another layer of bureaucracy.

Two key strategic developments, which were significant external drivers for WYLLN, occurred in 2009. Firstly the establishment of Employment and Skills Boards within each of the five local authorities within West Yorkshire, with the statutory requirement to produce a three year Work and Skills Plan for April 2010 to March 2014. Secondly, in November 2009, the launch of the Leeds City Region, as the economic unit within the region, which comprises of eleven local authority areas including all West Yorkshire authorities. These developments would provide both infrastructure and strategy directives against which WYLLN could position and further develop its higher level skills business engagement strategy and practice.

Following discussions with Leeds City Region representatives, local councillors and officers within each of the five local authorities, Business Link, and with WYLLN partner institutions, the WYLLN Board approved the funding for five Higher Level Skills Coordinators.

Local Arrangements

Higher Level Skills Coordinators (HLSC) were established in each local authority area in West Yorkshire and positioned in order to support and influence the local Employment and Skills Boards. This resulted in four HLSC each being located within Bradford, Calderdale, Kirklees and Wakefield local authorities, reporting into economy and regeneration directorates, and one HLSC being located within the Chamber of Commerce of Leeds.

Due to the distinct contexts of respective host organisations and local agendas the individual HLSC have delivered in different ways. Those located within council directorates have provided substantial input to strategic initiatives guided by regeneration and economic development issues and working with key account staff and key accounts of the council. In Leeds the HLSC has had greater direct contact with the business community via the Chamber networks and has been able to contribute to practical business development outcomes such as training delivery, progression agreements from in-company training and a range of employer-based training accreditations.

Outcomes were established and agreed for each HLSC and these included targets for engagement, progression agreements and accreditation. Soft targets were agreed that included network development, local market intelligence gathering and communication and development of demand for higher level skills.

Each HLSC gained a seat at the local Employment & Skills Board and instigated business surveys to ascertain opinion on employment and skills issues and from these formed focus groups to explore issues more deeply. The information gained from this activity was fed back to both the local Employment & Skills Boards and to WYLLN partners via WYLLN communications and delivery of presentations at WYLLN meetings and conferences.

Higher Level Skills Coordinators Operation and Practice

The HLSC operated within a complex environment in that the role sat as a conduit between businesses, agencies, the WYLLN central team and individual partner institutions. As 'honest brokers' it was important to recognise the different perspectives of the stakeholders concerned whilst maintaining the critical recognition that WYLLN funded the HLSC and therefore expected a return for the WYLLN partners.

The key product offered by the HLSC network was a non-biased brokerage service that enabled businesses and agencies to link with the WYLLN partners. One of the ongoing frustrations, regularly reported to WYLLN from business in relation to FE Colleges (FEC) and Higher Education Institutions (HEI), is that of being able to access the right people within FEC and HEI and the HLSC network aimed to alleviate this difficulty.

In addition, the networks and connections that the HLSCs secured enabled gathering of intelligence from businesses and agencies in relation to current and future skills needs and the ability to share this intelligence with the WYLLN central team and WYLLN partner institutions. Equally flow of intelligence from WYLLN partners to businesses and agencies was enabled.

The cost of establishing the HLSC roles was significant and drawn from the WYLLN grant. In addition, in-kind contributions were made by each of the local authorities. As such no direct cost was incurred by WYLLN partners or businesses and agencies. This therefore enabled a period of experimentation and service provision that had previously been missing within the higher skills landscape.

Limited budget existed for major promotion of the service available and therefore marketing materials were limited to a small tri-fold business card. Additionally, existing WYLLN marketing material was available for use for example, sector booklets, coordinated CPD publications etc. The key mechanism used to promote services to business was personal engagement between the HLSC and the networks available within their specific areas, for example WYLLN sector groups, chamber networks, council key accounts, Business Link, Leeds City Region groups, manufacturing alliances, training networks etc.

Key contacts were identified within each WYLLN partner and in the main this worked well. However as with all such arrangements some contacts performed better than others with a range of responses from rapid and positive, through to patchy and on to non-existent. As the HLSC was the visible contact for the business the 'non-responses' were hidden from the business and as such the impression to business was always positive with every referral receiving at least one positive partner response and within short timeframes.

From the outset WYLLN Directors worked with the HLSC in establishing a model of engagement. This involved a clear recognition that the HLSC represented the full network and therefore acted as 'honest brokers' promoting opportunities to all WYLLN partners. In addition a code of practice was established at the early stages of tenure that set out key ethical principles of operation.

Early in operations the need for more transparent communications and sharing of intelligence between the HLSC was recognised. Without a true customer relationship management (CRM) system being available across locations the use of GoogleDocs was established with a common spreadsheet capturing headline business engagements. More detail was then captured on a system of tracking documents including:

- **Contact sheet** containing details of the organisation, sector, outline of discussions, potential services of interest, actions required and deadlines for actions to be completed. All subsequent contacts being recorded in order to track the relationship

- **Referral sheet** detailing specific opportunities for WYLLN partners to respond to again stipulating deadline for completion of responses

- **EBTA referral sheets** for those engagements requesting an EBTA proposal.

- **Evaluation sheets** for capturing business opinion of the level of service offered by both the HLSC and the WYLLN partners responding to referrals

Achievements

The soft targets set have progressed with development of an increased profile for the WYLLN amongst businesses and key agencies, a degree of embedding within key networks across West Yorkshire and improved levels of intelligence, not only in relation to higher level skills needs, but skills in general and local market intelligence.

Table 15.1: Summary of Activity and Outcomes for Higher Level Skills Coordinators

Activity	Outcomes
Business Engagements	Over 10,000
Meaningful Business Engagements	140
Referrals to WYLLN Partners	56
Referral Responses from WYLLN Partners	56
Activity/Contracts Secured by WYLLN Partners	1 Economic Challenge Investment Fund intervention. 3 Charity events supported. 2 Student projects secured. 3 Student placement opportunities. 1 Online learning development supported. 1 media practice opportunity secured. Numerous introductions provided and information shared.
Work Based Progression Agreements	6 Completed 69 Potential in pipeline.

Activity	Outcomes
Employer-based Training Accreditations	1 Fully completed
	7 full proposals offered. 6 businesses declined on grounds of costs and public sector funding cuts. 1 proposal was still under consideration.
Contributions to Strategic Documents/Policy	Coalition Government employment and skills consultations contributed to via British Chamber of Commerce responses.
	Local Employment & Skills Board policies influenced.
	LCR Employment & Skills Board policies influenced.
	Contribution to economic growth strategy for Wakefield.
Contributions to Development of Bids	LCR Employment & Skills Board RGF bid supported.
	ERDF bids in Calderdale and Wakefield supported.
Staff Development Offered	'Getting Engaged for Delivery', sharing experiences of HLSC and developing new ways of working.
	'Realising Scattered Commonalities', sharing the key differences between authority areas but equally the common themes.
	Non-formal staff development input to partners via localised engagement.
Employer Surveys and Focus Groups Undertaken	Leeds Chamber survey developed and deployed.
	6 employer focus groups held with Leeds Chamber members.
	Bradford; Calderdale and Wakefield skills surveys developed and deployed.
Other	HLSC supported central WYLLN team in developing a business offer of short courses by HE providers and the development of a business facing website providing this offer.

Conclusions

- A large number of businesses engaged by the HLSC had pre-existing links with HE providers and where this was the case the vast majority were satisfied with the service and quality received. It was noted however that a considerable number of such businesses were unaware of the full range of services that their provider could offer

- Businesses were highly appreciative of the HLSC who were seen as independent and autonomous sources of information in relation to skills advice, access to the regions providers, navigation through the skills system, explanation of the levels and providing guidance in relation to the range of services available from the providers. This contrasted significantly to the negative comments relating to approaches to individual providers that were perceived to have weak businesses facing websites and contact arrangements and less than helpful reception processes. Although the HLSC role was envisaged to support higher level skills initiatives businesses equally appreciated the network offering support for accessing lower level skills via the FEC partners

- A sizeable majority of businesses engaged, both those with pre-existing relationships and those without, had strong perceptions that private providers of training are more fleet of foot and able to customise their services than those from the public sector and a number consider them to be better value for money. A number of businesses expressed exasperation at public funding for training schemes, for example Train to Gain, stating that their experiences dissuaded them from engaging with such schemes citing the bureaucracy as being horrendous

- Businesses consider the practice of including set on-costs to the price as being outdated and the level involved expensive. There is an expectation that institutions should be able to apply marginal costing. Equally, businesses have unrealistic expectations of prices from 'public sector' providers as compared to private providers, that is, they expect the public sector to be considerably lower cost than private providers

- Accreditation of in-house training was very difficult to pursue as the costs associated with accreditation have been prohibitive, even from WYLLN partners who have a marginal costing model. The costs associated are predicated on a model of quality assurance that tends to be heavy handed

- The value of the HLSC brokering and drafting progression agreements has been substantial, especially in securing multiple entry and exit agreements. Progression agreements have been particularly valued by training providers and have enabled them to enter into relationships with FEC and higher education institutions (HEI) resulting in recruitment of learners for the FEC and HEI. Those FEC and HEI offering progression opportunities that include a 'credit allowance' for training undertaken with the training providers have proved more successful than those without. The lower costs involved in establishing progression agreements as compared to EBTA is seen as a strong potential recruitment route

- The connections with local and Leeds City Region Employment & Skills Boards have heightened awareness of the range of services available from FEC and HEI. The flow of information from these boards in relation to business and regional need has been supported via the links with WYLLN

Learning Outcomes

- HE providers need to consider relationship and brand management and the need to 'cross sell' services to existing clients

- Post compulsory education providers are recommended to review their business facing approaches to ensure that information relating to services to business are clear and unambiguous, that their websites enable rapid access to business support information and that reception staff are trained to offer a commercial level of service. In regions with numerous providers it is also recommended that providers consider forming a partnership and share the costs for business engagement activities, effectively offering a semi-autonomous and single point of contact for businesses

- In light of the changes to funding arrangements, providers should not be afraid of charging commercial fees provided that the speed of response and quality of service and delivery are sound

- HE providers need to lighten the touch and reduce the resource expended in relation to course approval and this in turn should result in savings for main stream course approval too

- HE providers are urged to consider development of progression agreements that offer credit allowance for in-house and training provider programmes as a means to recruitment of learners from the workplace

CHAPTER 16

Overcoming the Quality Assurance Challenges Faced by HE Provision in an Employer-based Environment

Frank Haddleton, Director of Academic Quality Assurance and Enhancement, University of Hertfordshire

Ann Minton, Workforce Development Fellow, University of Derby

Introduction

Most universities now offer some form of service to employers to allow the delivery of accredited training, but the nature of that provision varies tremendously:

- It could be the (i) delivery of off-the-shelf university provision, (ii) university-developed provision bespoke to the employer, (iii) accreditation of the company's own provision or (iv) the accreditation of the provision of private training providers for delivery to a range of customers

- It could involve the delivery of small packages of standalone credit or provide for a range of awards (from 'small' CPD awards to larger traditional awards such as Foundation Degrees or Bachelors Degrees)

- In some cases the employer or training provider conducts all assessments, whereas other universities take responsibility for all summative assessment, or there is shared responsibility

In each variation of provision there are challenges to be overcome in terms of the initiation of the partnership, development of the provision, development of the provider, approval of the provision and ongoing quality assurance processes. These challenges are magnified by the expectations of the Quality Assurance Agency (QAA)

Academic Infrastructure (2008), which was not originally developed with employer-based provision in mind and needs further articulation to clarify its application to this environment.

Drawing on the experience of two demonstrator projects (Whitemore and Minton, 2010 and Haddleton, 2010) which collated the experience of a number of partner universities in the areas of designing bespoke provision and accreditation of in-company training, we have developed a model for consideration by those who are considering the development of processes and procedure for employer responsive provision.

We identify 3 key areas of focus The 3 P's for Employer Engagement:

- People

- Processes

- Practice.

Each area underpins the actions of the others and thus a holistic approach to employer engagement and specifically accreditation of in-company provision is promoted within a university in which employer engagement activity is embedded within the core values and mission of the institution.

This chapter therefore

- Examines the varied nature of employer-based provision and the different quality assurance challenges that arise from each

- Identifies aspects of the QAA Academic Infrastructure (2008) that offer particular challenges to this form of provision

- Discusses the potential incompatibilities between employer expectations and HE quality assurance expectations

- Identifies how these challenges are being overcome, in terms of the development of such provision and its approval

Background

It is critically important that HE programmes are explicitly located within the QAA Academic Infrastructure and can demonstrate that they operate within a robust framework for the assurance of quality and standards. It is this quality framework that ensures that there is parity in the standard of provision amongst all UK universities and offers creditability to qualifications.

QAA have identified the following quality assurance considerations related to employer-responsive provision (QAA, Feb 2010, para 38)

- The types of partnerships and the corresponding forms of agreements required

- The setting and maintaining of academic standards

- The quality of the learning opportunities provided to students

- The involvement of employers and learners in the design, delivery and assessment of learning.

Leitch (2006) recommended that universities needed to work closely with employers to ensure that the workforce had access to the provision of higher education to meet the skills and development needs for the economic growth of the country, given that the majority of those in need of HE were already in the workplace. It is clear that 'more of the same', traditionally taught full time or day release courses, would not address these needs, and more innovative solutions were called for. Specifically required (Tallantyre, 2010 p.46) were highly flexible approaches in relation to

- Content that was more negotiated with employers and employees

- Situated in the workplace, or at least off-campus

- Delivered at a distance or through technology

- At times and pace to suit the learners

- With forms of assessment perceived as relevant to work activity

- Based on more generic learning outcomes

- Collected into shorter credit or award bearing packages: so called 'bite sized provision.

Thus, when accrediting in-company provision the people, processes and practices must be underpinned by the principles of HE Quality Assurance.

Variations in Employer-based Provision and the QA Challenges Arising

The development of credit-bearing short awards, encouraging learners to develop their knowledge, competence and skills by engaging in the workplace with learning opportunities related to the principles and practices of their work, can bring HE within the workplace and employment within the HE curriculum. Such programmes will vary in terms of their academic level and volume of credit. The Higher Education

Academy (HEA) Work-based Learning Impact Study (Nixon, 2008) acknowledges the value that employers and employees placed on short HE programmes of only 30 credits. However, there is still demand by employers for full programmes of study leading to major awards as indicated by the success of Foundation Degrees, and subsequent progression to full honours awards.

Programmes vary significantly across different awarding institutions (Whitemore & Minton 2010; Haddleton 2010), from the accreditation of standalone credit to the validation of large awards, from 4 credit-points to 360 credit points, from delivery of off-the-shelf university provision to accreditation of the company's own provision and from policies of the company carrying out all assessments to the awarding institution taking responsibility for all assessment. Similar challenges are faced across these spectra, although to differing extents. In some circumstances the QAA Academic Infrastructure seems entirely appropriate; in others they can be likened to 'a sledgehammer to crack a nut'.

Processes

For Employer Engagement activity to be successful it needs to be recognised and valued by the university as being of equal standing to traditional Undergraduate and Postgraduate provision and research activity, rather than as a peripheral offer, and as such the processes for approval and monitoring should be rigorous but not onerous, reflecting the risk and proportionality principle.

QAA has also recognised that the processes used for employer-based provision may need to be modified, and the need for both responsiveness and proportionality were key factors:

> '...responsiveness (in terms of approval of provision, award of credit); recognition of the scale of provision (often small amounts of credit, as opposed to whole programmes of study).'

> 'The process should have the same rigour, but arriving at this state by different means. The whole system has to be sufficiently flexible in order to meet employer and institutional needs. Quality assurance has to meet the complexity and flexibility of:

> a) negotiated learning, the timing of delivery, start and end dates etc

> b) negotiated provision with the employer and the learner.'

> '...the challenge of balancing appropriate oversight with the speed of responsiveness employers want.'

> (QAA, Feb 2010 para 29)

Approval mechanisms should be founded on QAA precepts but tailored to meet the need of this type of provision, for example the use of a shell framework, with delegated powers of approval (Whitemore and Minton, 2010). Where awarding institutions are approving major awards, the processes used are often essentially the same as those for validated collaborative programmes i.e. programme validation and periodic revalidation, with external involvement. The approval of smaller awards relating to in-company provision often apply streamlined approval processes (see case studies from Derby, Harper Adams and Wolverhampton) but essentially all quality assurance issues are covered. Most awarding institutions have paper-based processes for the approval of standalone credit, with external involvement as appropriate (Whitemore & Minton 2010).

Proportionality is evidenced in a tiered or differential approach in some institutions based on the volume of credit and the level of the credit, with a standing panel of external examiners/advisers being asked to review proposals. Other institutions utilise a preapproved set of generic learning outcomes or short course descriptors, which also addresses the issue of externality as part of the approvals mechanism (Whitemore & Minton, 2010; Haddleton, 2010).

The approval arrangements for tri-partite agreements (that is, where an awarding institution approves a training provider to deliver courses to a company) will vary according to the individual nature of the agreement and who 'owns' the course.

- If a company owns the intellectual property rights (IPR) to a course and then contracts one or more training providers to deliver that course, then the company would need to be approved (along with its courses and resources), and the training providers would be approved by the university through confirming the acceptability of CVs. A teaching staff qualifications policy is essential in these situations

- However, if a training provider owns the IPR and delivers the same course to several companies, the university would normally approve the provider only. The approval process for the delivery site would depend on the nature of the course and the physical resource requirements. If all that is required is a teaching room to deliver the course then this responsibility could be delegated to the training provider (however some universities do still insist on approving the site in this situation)

Practice

Accepted good practice, derived from experience with both short awards (Whitemore and Minton 2010) and Foundation Degrees, notes that employers **have** to be involved in the identification and scoping of the curriculum, including the identification of relevant professional or industry benchmarks that can be aligned to the curriculum. Experience (Whitemore &, Minton, 2010) from working with companies ranging in size from large multinational companies to SMEs, suggests that in each case contextualisation of the curriculum within the workplace is vital for success for both learners and employers. Where the assessment is based on real work activity, this is felt to have greater impact on the organisation (Nixon, 2008). Furthermore, having a 'champion' within the workplace to whom learners can refer was found to be valuable in ensuring that potential barriers within the employer organisation could be quickly identified and overcome before they became a problem to the learners.

A key to successful curriculum development was considered to lie in having a lead academic and lead developer in the partner to ensure that it remains fit for purpose in terms of the requirements of the employer and the standards of the university (Bolden, Connor, Duquemin, Hirsh. and Petrov, 2009). Furthermore, academic staff should support the articulation of the agreed curriculum with the partner by aligning it to HE standards, together with shaping the assessment so that it is relevant **and** rigorous as well as founded in real work activity (Boud and Solomon, 2001). Aligning the provision to the Framework for Higher Education Qualifications (FHEQ) (QAA, Aug 2008), by the ascription of credit and level, is fundamental to ensuring that the provision is clearly characterised as higher education, and thus distinguished from other training providers. Due consideration should be given to relevant external reference points (National Occupational Standards; Professional or Statutory-Regulatory Bodies; QAA benchmark statements). As with more traditional or conventional provision this is likely to be an integral part of the approval of the programme, to ensure academic consistency and to facilitate the assimilation of academic practices and administration procedures, whilst maintaining the operational context and business focus. This is often achieved by embedding the statements within framework, programme and/or module learning outcomes, whilst recognising that the QAA benchmark statements do not intend to prescribe the content of the curriculum, but to provide a sound basis on which to align key areas of study. These are in the realm of the academic and it is important that those involved in the discussion with employers are able to explain the need to harmonise provision with these key requirements and HE characteristics. The mapping of in-company training to FHEQ and QAA subject benchmarks is generally carried out at the developmental stage of approval. However, FHEQ is often a more useful benchmark than subject benchmark statements at this stage. The translation of subject benchmark statements into work-based learning outcomes was seen to be more difficult than translating into traditional programme outcomes, often because the levels of credit typically involved are only likely to satisfy a small proportion of the subject benchmark statements in a discipline.

Some HEIs report (Haddleton 2010; Whitemore and Minton, 2010) that the use of Credit Level Descriptors (e.g. SEEC, 2010) leads to greater consistency in approach to learning outcomes and standards of short course provision, thus ensuring that there is parity with other provision within the university and other negotiated WBL programmes across the country.

Staff development is essential for all involved in employer engagement activity (university and partner staff) on an on-going basis. This will include discussion about best practice in curriculum design, assessment and quality assurance for all those involved in the employer-HE relationship. This should be undertaken on an on-going basis, regularly reviewing the provision, to identify best practice to share across the institution, and being involved in the dissemination of best practice to and from other institutions.

People

High level support at Vice Chancellor, Deputy Vice-Chancellor, Pro Vice Chancellor, Dean, Chief Executive and Senior Manager level is essential, so that key decision makers can influence the wider university systems and company systems to develop an infrastructure that supports and enables a proactive response to employers and the university. This is supported in the findings of a joint study from Council for Industry and Higher Education (CIHE) and the University of Exeter (Bolden et al, 2009).

Key staff are needed at both institutional and faculty management level, to ensure that the organisational infrastructure will enable employer engagement activity to work for employers. They are also needed at programme level to ensure that employer needs are genuinely being met, rather than repackaging existing provision for the convenience of the university. Work based learning and employer engagement should be valued equally with other teaching and learning and research activity. It is important to employ and develop academics who are comfortable and familiar with working with employers, understanding their needs and the way that they work. These academics need to understand academic quality mechanisms and key benchmarks, and to be able to 'translate' and 'harmonise' between employers and academia in the development phase.

Whitemore and Minton (2010) found that for successful employer engagement activity key liaison staff should be identified within the support departments of the university (Registry, Quality, IT, Library,) to ensure that the infrastructure supports the needs of the accredited employer-based provision both in terms of processes for approval and for implementation.

Whitemore and Minton (2010) indicate that there also needs to be a key contact for the employer who will act as a liaison between the two organisations and champion the programme within the organisation. They too need to be supported by an executive level sponsor who will overcome barriers and demonstrate to potential learners that the employer values the qualification. This is particularly important where the accreditation of in-company training is being considered to ensure that the collaborative processes of the university are managed slickly and efficiently.

The use of external academic staff involved in course approval varies across awarding institutions, and will depend upon whether awards or standalone credit are being delivered. In some awarding institutions, an external member with knowledge of the work-based environment would be used, through appointment to an accreditation board. These external members have experience in work-based learning as they are assuring the quality of the learning, not of any subject. The subject-specific content would be assured by a specialist link advisor who acts as an external member to the employer's assessment process (and is a member of the accreditation board), or alternatively a subject external member would additionally provide commentary on the curriculum to the approval panel. However, other awarding institutions insist on the use of external members with specialist knowledge of the discipline being approved (on the basis that one of the external's primary functions is to approve the standard of the proposed courses). The former approach is more likely to be used for the significant proportion of in-company training which tends to focus on leadership and management skills of employees; as experienced academics these externals typically have an understanding of the level of skills required. However, for award/credit of a specialist nature then knowledge of the discipline is paramount. For instance, the standard of a Master's-level credit-rated short course for doctors and surgeons in advanced practice techniques could not be judged by a non-subject specialist external.

Conclusion

Quality assurance issues relating to university-level provision developed for and with employers are critical to the employer engagement agenda. For the education to be recognised and valued both by the sector and the employers, the quality assurance mechanisms must reflect the expectations of Higher Education generally. Clearly, quality assurance processes for such activity must be robust, the university 'imprimatur' is why employers are engaging with HE rather than with a training provider. However, in order to meet business requirements and timescales, these processes should be proportionate, fit-for-purpose and not constrained by the accepted assumptions of procedures designed for full-time students.

Key Learning Points

- The **Processes** of the university need to be founded in the QAA Academic infrastructure, but need to be sufficiently flexible to meet the needs of the accreditation of in company provision, which is often of low credit tariff and results in the achievement of minor awards. Partner organisations need to recognise that the value of the accreditation comes from this infrastructure and be willing to adopt and adapt provision without comprising satisfaction of meeting the business need (see Derby/Croda case study, Chapter 4)

- The **Practice** in approving in-company provision needs to reflect the ethos and principles of work based learning, by applying learning in the workplace and using real work for assessment activity. This means adapting current practice to meet the needs of the partner (for both the university and the organisation). It also means that the programme must be valued and championed within both organisations

- The **People** involved in such provision need to have an understanding of the work based learning agenda. Academics need to be willing to understand the context of the organisation and understand their language and people from the organisation must be willing to engage with some of the HE language, if they are to truly facilitate HE, rather than be deliverers of knowledge. Above all there needs to be a multidisciplinary, multi-level interface (beyond the academic and the trainer) to make partnership really work and get the best out of the partnership for all involved

References

Boud, D. and Solomon, N. (eds) (2001) *Work Based Learning: a New Higher Education?* Buckingham: SRHE & Open University Press

Bolden, R., Connor, H., Duquemin, A., Hirsh, W. and Petrov, G. (2009) *Employer Engagement with Higher Education: Defining Sustaining and Supporting Higher Skills Provision.* London CIHE

Haddleton, F., (2010) *Accreditation of In-company Programmes* York, Higher Education Academy

Leitch, S. (2006) *Prosperity for All in the Global Economy – World Class Skills (Leitch Review of Skills)* December DfES

Nixon, I. (ed) (2008) Work Based Learning Impact Study York The Higher Education Academy

QAA (Feb 2010) *Employer-responsive provision survey: A reflective report.* Available at http://www.qaa.ac.uk/employers/EffectiveProvision.pdf

QAA (Oct 2010) Code of practice for the assurance of academic quality and standards in Higher Education. Section 2: *Collaborative provision and flexible and distributed learning (including e-learning)* – Amplified version October 2010. Available at http://www.qaa.ac.uk/academicinfrastructure/codeOfPractice/section2/collab2010.pdf (accessed 29/3/2011)

QAA (Aug 2008) *The framework for higher education qualifications in England, Wales and Northern Ireland*, August 2008 (FHEQ). Available at http://www.qaa.ac.uk/academicinfrastructure/FHEQ/EWNI08/FHEQ08.pdf (accessed 11/04/2011)

QAA (Sept 2006) Code of practice for the assurance of academic quality and standards in Higher Education. Section 6: *Assessment of students*. Available at http://www.qaa.ac.uk/academicinfrastructure/codeOfPractice/section6/COP_AOS.pdf (accessed 11/04/2011)

SEEC (2010) *Credit level descriptors for Higher Education.* Available at http://www.seec.org.uk/sites/seec.org.uk/files/SEEC%20Level%20Descriptors%202010_0.pdf (accessed 11/04/2011)

Tallentyre, F. (2010) *Foreword to* Whitemore, D. & Minton, A (2010) A *Rapid Response and Fit For Purpose Solutions for Employers, Which Maintain Standards* York HEA

Whitemore, D. & Minton, A. (2010) A *Rapid Response and Fit For Purpose Solutions for Employers, Which Maintain Standards* York HEA

Willis, K. (2008) *Frameworks for Work-based Learning* in Tallantyre, F. (ed) (2008)*Workforce development: Connections, Frameworks and Processes,* York: Higher Education Academy

CHAPTER 17

'Courtship Underpinned by Audit': Challenges and Solutions in Quality Assuring Employer Responsive Provision

Lydia Arnold, Liz Warr and Charles Cowap, Harper Adams University College

Executive Summary

As HEIs engage with employers to deliver programmes that are partially or wholly based in the workplace they face new challenges in quality assuring provision that may be geographically or corporately remote These should be delivered in bite-sized chunks and not naturally aligned with the academic year or with the traditional relationships between tuition, subject specialisms, resourcing, tutoring, assessment, peer review and academic quality assurance. This chapter focuses on the challenges and issues of quality assuring employer focused higher-level provision.

Employer responsive provision at Harper Adams University College is particularly characterised by the prevalence of SMEs, small credit volumes, the integration of industry standards and distributed delivery. The quality assurance landscape must therefore be accommodating and flexible. Reflecting the view that quality assurance and enhancement occurs across the life a programme, from course design to external review, the chapter uses stages in the life cycle of a typical employer engagement initiative to structure a consideration of the mechanisms used by the College to assure the quality of its provision.

Conclusions are drawn about the importance of partners getting to know each other and the role of professional trust and confidence. In addition the development of a positive staff culture around work-based learning is also highlighted. The role of experts in building confidence and competence for employer responsive provision is an emerging theme throughout.

Introduction

Harper Adams University College has seen a rapid expansion of its Employer Responsive Provision (ERP) since 2008. This chapter presents the College's approach to the assurance of standards and enhancement of academic quality at each stage in the development of new ERP proposals, from project initiation and design through to monitoring and review.

The Harper Adams Context

Harper Adams has developed an eclectic portfolio of employer engagements (see Figure 17.1), much of it through the REEDNet (Rural Employer Engagement Development Network) project (see Arnold, Warr and Newlyn, 2010). This diverse provision, with different patterns of remote delivery, work-based assessment and industrial involvement has created challenges for quality assurance and enhancement arrangements.

Figure 17.1: Examples of Harper Adams University College's accredited ERP

- Animal medicines training for the relevant regulatory authority (AMTRA)
- University College Foundation Certificate in Professional Skills for Overseas Development in partnership with an international volunteering charity
- Postgraduate Certificates developed for individuals working in rural business
- Farm skills in dairy herd management delivered by veterinary surgeons
- University Foundation Certificate in Commercial Harness Horse Driving delivered by a further education college and a professional body
- Master's in Veterinary Physiotherapy delivered with the relevant professional body

In its 2010 QAA audit Harper Adams was specifically praised for 'the development of employer-linked provision through an approach that seeks to integrate it with the College's other collaborative provision in respect of quality assurance requirements' (QAA, 2010a, p.14).

A number of overarching principles have shaped approaches to quality assuring ERP at the College:

- Approaches are based on the existing QAA's *Quality Assurance Framework*. Sometimes this may require novel application to avoid what Haddleton (2010) refers to as 'a sledgehammer cracking a nut'
- The purpose of quality assurance is to safeguard academic standards

- The varying nature and scale of ERP mean that innovative approaches are required to meet the individual needs of employers while remaining cost effective for the HEI (QAA, 2010b)

- Quality assurance (QA) for ERP should be proportionate (Haddleton, 2010)

- HEIs and employers are best placed to determine effective mechanisms for QA from professional and academic perspectives

- HEIs are responsible for their own robust internal quality assurance processes

- External examiners should be used where necessary to provide comparative judgments on standards (Ambrose and Ni Luanaigh, 2009)

The approach taken has been based on the belief that academic standards and quality can, and should, be assured and enhanced on a continuous basis throughout the programme life-cycle.

Project Initiation and Design

Quality expectations are formulated early in the relationship between employers and HEIs through the development of mutual understanding and respect. Personnel involved at this stage are crucial. The quality of early development work, and all that flows from it, can be raised by the involvement of experts to support development managers and academics. Such individuals must have a good understanding of higher education systems and the ability to communicate effectively with academic staff and employers (Eyres, Hooker, and Pringle, 2008). The involvement of experts enables the identification and resolution of potential threats to academic standards early in the design process. At Harper Adams, a core team of specialists work across the institution to engender consistency of judgment and their engagement in external forums has provided additional insight and alignment. Two different employers describe the value of specific work-based learning personnel to the process of design and accreditation here:

'There is no chance that accreditation would ever had got off the ground without the support of a work based learning team to guide us in the right direction, reassure us and give us confidence that the process would be successful. Harper also had ...an understanding of where our current training could be pitched (in terms of credits and level).'

'Without the drive and enthusiasm of the WBL team, there would have been no partnership formation. The ability of the designated programme leader... undoubtedly smoothed the way to the development of the partnership and the understanding of the curriculum development team has further enhanced the partnership.'

In the formation of new partnerships early definition of respective responsibilities is vital. Comprehensive analysis of the components of an employer engagement arrangement ensures that the most appropriate partner assumes responsibility for each.

A detailed template has been designed to define arrangements for curriculum design and delivery, student support and guidance, assessment, learning resources, quality assurance and enhancement. It also includes a risk assessment component. The template comprises a list of 67 points for consideration (for an example see Figure 17.2). The template appears daunting but the specialist team takes on responsibility for populating it. This comprehensive analysis is reassuring for the institution. It provides clarity of the responsibilities associated with provision for partners and enables them to articulate their own support needs, while at the same time enlarging their understanding of HE requirements through dialogue. This completed template forms the basis of the ERP contract documentation.

Figure 17.2: An extract from one aspect of a planning template (addressing arrangements for approving trainers, mentors and assessors)

Approval process for trainers, mentors, assessors

All trainers are experienced practitioners and therefore have an understanding of the issues encountered by learners (example CVs attached). Trainers must evidence criteria established by ABS to gain their appointment.

The ABS criteria for trainer appointments include:

- At Least 1 year's experience training adults in diversity groups
- 2 years' professional experience
- At least 2 years' experience working in development overseas
- Experience in giving presentations to groups (both small and large)
- Current knowledge of international development issues
- Experience of
    - o   Recognising and working with diversity
    - o   Designing and developing training sessions
    - o   Facilitating group learning activities with adults
    - o   Evaluating and developing own training practice
    - o   Managing relationships with colleagues in a training context
- Ability to draw on experience and give relevant examples to reinforce volunteer learning.

ABS will be responsible for collating and forwarding the up to date CVs of delivery staff to the link tutor to be reviewed annually.

Assessors will be selected from the trainer pool. Assessors have had sufficient time available to fulfill the role and must be HE qualified and willing to engage in developmental sessions. The assessors will be ABS and the link tutor. CVs of assessors will be retained by the link tutor.

Partners have observed that this approach reflects the seriousness of the commitment and provides the chance to think through how arrangements will work in practice. Partners also acknowledge the role of the core team in facilitating dialogue, documenting the outcomes and asking probing questions. One employer reported:

'At the time of the approval, the pace of development increased significantly as the approval date approached ... [we] invested trust in the [Harper Adams] lead person and were not let down ... The value of the approval form has been in retrospect, in that it clearly states roles and responsibilities for the programme'.

Recognising that this definitive master documentation is dense it can be selectively and purposefully re-presented; for example it can inform a process flow diagram detailing who is responsible for what action or provision at each point in the student journey. One partner found this particularly valuable:

'I did find the flow chart helpful, as it was useful to have a visual representation of whose responsibility lies where at each stage of the process'.

This approach aligns with voices captured in the QAA's *Employer-responsive provision survey (QAA, 2010b),* which suggest that institutions can delegate teaching and learning provided that the partner has the capacity to manage that learning. The dialogue generated by these processes engenders confidence that where a partner is assuming a particular responsibility they are able to meet their obligations.

Whilst employers wish to influence the scale and content of provision and often seek to develop a named award they are not always explicitly concerned about the level or volume of credit assigned to it. HEIs must employ academic judgment to determine these parameters in order to achieve parity and explain to employers the principles underpinning their decisions. National qualification and credit frameworks are crucial reference points in such conversations.

The involvement of independent individuals in the debate can be helpful in providing a degree of objectivity to such discussions.

Programme Approval

The need for flexibility and rapidity in developing and approving new ERP has been widely stated (see for example, Whitemore and Minton, 2010). At Harper Adams a monthly accreditation and validation committee has ensured swiftness and has enabled panel members to develop shared understandings of work-based learning (see Figure 17.3).

Figure 17.3: Illustrative quote from a member of the Employer Engagement Accreditation and Validation Committee

'Early in the committee's life we were very cautious, but as we have moved on we have undertaken a great deal of discussion about where risks may lie, what real risks are and what contingencies we may hold. The committee's single focus on employer engagements has given us an area to undertake deep scrutiny but also to develop our own understandings ... The trust built up amongst the committee has enabled frank and challenging discussions and learning from our own prior experience'.

The participation of industry and academic partners in validation meetings has enhanced confidence in proposals and helped to develop committee members' understanding of the context of planned provision. The presence of external representatives was initially challenging, but through collective learning around conduct, scheduling and the place of open and closed sessions, partner representation at validations has become routine and beneficial to the speedy resolution of issues arising.

Clearly defined module specifications with appropriate learning outcomes and detailed teaching, learning and assessment strategies enable committee members to make informed judgments about academic standards and quality. The module descriptor, far from a being a paper ticket to validation, is seen as a living document that serves to standardise practice across partners. It is important that appropriate use is made of qualification and level descriptors derived from the Framework for Higher Education Qualifications when writing this documentation to ensure parity across accredited provision.

Delivery and Assessment

The time-scale for delivery and assessment is more likely to coincide with the employer's processes rather than the cycle of the academic year, affecting learning, teaching and assessment strategies. Workplace support for this type of learning is vital; the use of mentors and /or supervisors is common.

Harper Adams is working closely with individuals delivering, assessing and supporting ERP to bring about a deep understanding of academic quality assurance in higher education and the time required for its attainment. A 'Train the Trainer' model is emerging. For example, a module 'Training HE Trainers' has been accredited and used as a module to extend the learning on the Sector Skills Council approved

'Instructional Techniques' course. This has been delivered to the veterinary surgeons delivering Farm Skills modules, involving them in designing assignments for use in the distributed delivery of these courses. Similarly 'Developing the role of the Clinical Educator' is used to train Veterinary Physiotherapists offering placements. In course evaluation participants agreed that they felt more confident and able to offer student placements after the course which highlighted theory, practice and knowledge to put a placement programme together. They felt better equipped to progress as clinical educators.

Beyond initial training, partners are invited to join teaching and learning events run quarterly in the University College and frequent reviews enable a discussion around training needs of partner staff. Harper Adams has also invested in staff training events to ensure standardisation of assessment decisions. For example, workshops have been held to standardise nation-wide assessment procedures and criteria for the modules run in conjunction with the Animal Medicines Trading Regulatory Authority (AMTRA), the BASIS Crop Protection Scheme and Voluntary Service Overseas (VSO). Of these workshops one employer partner said:

> 'It was ... very important for us that Harper were able to deliver a workshop for our assessors and arrange a follow up calibration meeting to ensure we were working to the same standards'.

The historic tendency to retain tight control over delivery aspects has been relaxed and decisions about responsibility for delivery are made on the grounds of who is best placed, most expert and has capacity. Devolving assessment to partners requires a greater leap in faith although there is growing recognition that they may be best placed to assess elements of the curriculum that relate to specific industrial or professional competences. Furthermore, such elements of the curriculum may already be quality assured by the relevant professional body. The University College is increasingly acknowledging the validity of existing quality assurance mechanisms. For example, in provision developed for commercial harness horse drivers, the practical elements are taught and assessed by British Driving Society approved instructors and their decisions are ratified by the Society's Internal Verifiers. Participants maintain a reflective learning log and this is assessed by the partner college and scrutinised by the External Professional Reviewer appointed by Harper Adams. The partners assess relevant vocational competences and Harper Adams assesses the extended and meta-learning derived from concurrent experience in the work place.

Assessment and verification of work-based learning is through the development of competency-based objectives, using the 'novice to expert' model (Cowpe and Phillips, 2008). This may lead to an iterative assessment process, involving reflection and action planning, an approach particularly appropriate for extended periods of study, based on learning contracts rooted in the cultural and social environment of a particular place of work. Assessment is often through observation, interview or professional conversation. The most suitable assessor is often an industry professional rather than an academic and may be the workplace supervisor or line manager. It may be possible to integrate assessment processes into the individual's professional development and/or performance review cycle.

Higher-level learning requires that practice is underpinned by theory and the application of newly-acquired theory to subsequent practice. Reflection on this cycle lends itself more readily to quality assurance by the HEI or its nominated external representative and can embrace the individual's development assessed through workplace mechanisms. Across Harper Adams' ERP learning logs, reflective portfolios and discussions are used to tangibly capture learning through work.

Assessment of bite-sized learning presents similar issues as observations and professional conversations are again useful methodologies. There may be no permanent output from such assessment rendering conventional external examiner practice inadequate. It may be more appropriate to use industry experts in assessment (particularly for measurement of practical competencies) to ensure that successful achievement reflects the desired industry standard.

As with traditional programmes the quality of the learning environment and resources for learning is a key concern. The QAA's reflective report (2010b) suggested that in many partnership arrangements the ability of HEIs to exert control over the learning environment may be limited and that in such circumstances the HEI's bottom line responsibility is to ensure that the environment enables learners to meet intended learning outcomes and successfully complete their studies.

At Harper Adams it is now accepted that 'it is impossible to guarantee that each student will have exactly the same learning experience but you can ensure that each student has the opportunity to demonstrate and achieve the learning outcomes that have been set' (Stubbs, 2008). Fitness for purpose of learning environments and appropriateness and proportionality of resources are considered as part of the detailed planning process.

Monitoring and Review

External scrutiny is central to quality assurance. HEIs are expected to undertake their own internal reviews and draw upon the expertise of external examiners to provide comparative judgments on standards for all awards (SQW Consulting, 2008). QAA (2010b) identified a disparity of views about the appropriateness of the conventional external examiner role in ERP, particularly for small credit volumes, stand-alone modules and level four awards. Harper Adams has retained conventional external examiners for some of its ERP (generally for higher academic levels and larger credit volumes) but has also appointed external professional reviewers and professional advisors. The professional reviewer role is very similar to the conventional external reviewer, focusing primarily on the assessment process, but with greater emphasis on the professional capability of the individual. The professional advisor has a wider remit, looking at the currency and professional relevance of the curriculum, and seeking feedback from learners who are studying with a range of providers. One partner involved in delivering accredited Farm Skills Dairy modules, explains the value of this role:

> 'Having a professional advisor appointed, who is also a vet, to work with
> both parties has been reassuring: our trainers feel he is able to understand their
> background and working context and provide pragmatic and meaningful advice
> about how to transfer veterinary technical skills learning to our delegates in an
> accessible way'.

Traditional provision has formal internal monitoring arrangements (normally through a dedicated committee) and an equivalent process is required for ERP. A separate approach for ERP may be seen as losing the chance for cross-fertilisation of ideas, but the advantages of building a community of practitioners with a shared understanding of distributed work based learning are considerable and, it is suggested, outweigh the disadvantages. The Harper Adams Employer Engagement Course Committee has cross-institutional membership, enabling deep discussion of issues and comparison between employer engagement initiatives.

Feedback from key stakeholders (partner providers, employers, professional bodies and learners) is an important element of quality assurance, as is a mechanism for rapid institutional response. At Harper Adams different approaches are utilised, according to the nature and scale of the provision and contextual factors such as mode and sites of delivery, professional body involvement, number and type(s) of partner and use of learning technologies. Standardising feedback can be inappropriate, surveys may not be useful for a small cohort, perhaps far better to listen and discuss. Harper Adams has devised a review mechanism that encourages each course team to consider how it will gather feedback from its stakeholders. Standard themes are reviewed (such as quality of resources and learner satisfaction) whilst the methods to acquire feedback are not prescribed.

Conclusion

Comprehensive dialogue with partners is fundamental to developing mutual respect and understanding, and in ensuring that expectations of all parties are clear to all stakeholders. An approach of 'courtship underpinned by audit' ensures that all key aspects of provision are addressed in a thoughtful manner that is at the same time proportional to the approach adopted for traditional provision.

Our work has identified an overarching need for QA to be underpinned by a culture of mutual professional trust and confidence. The expertise of every partner must be acknowledged by the validating HEI and each given responsibility for the quality of their contribution when they are best placed to do so.

Lessons Learned

- Institutional confidence in collaborative ERP derives from detailed analysis of respective roles and responsibilities of all partners

- If Quality Assurance processes for ERP mirror those for conventional programmes it is easier to integrate them into institutional systems and structures

- 'Proportional' and 'equivalent' rather than 'identical' are appropriate terms to describe QA procedures for ERP in comparison to conventional provision

- Resistance to innovation in the quality assurance of ERP can, to a large extent, be overcome by cross-institutional involvement in approval, monitoring and review

- Experts who are active in the external work-based learning arena can have a major impact on quality assurance at each stage of the ERP programme life cycle, thus enhancing institutional confidence of the validating HEI

- Active participation of all key stake holders in their design, approval and review can enhance institutional confidence in creative ERP proposals

- Developing a community of practice in ERP is time-consuming but highly rewarding

References

Ambrose, P. and Ni Luanaigh, A. (2009) *Quality, Risk and Regulation: Collaborative provision and employer engagement in Higher education.* Viewpoint series: Issue 6, available at http://www.sqw.co.uk/file_download/188, accessed on 20th April 2010.

Arnold, L., Warr, L. and Newlyn, J. (2010) The Rural Employer Engagement Development Network: Lessons learned from the first year of the project in *Employer and Individual Demand for Higher Level Skills – The role of Higher Education. The abridged proceedings of The University Vocational Awards Council, York, 2010.* York: UVAC, pp.26–34.

Cowpe, M., and Phillips, D. (2008) Development of a degree work-based learning programme (Clinical Leadership): The Challenges of meeting the needs of employers and learners' in, *Higher Education Skills in the Workplace Delivering employer-led higher level work-based learning. The abridged proceedings of The University Vocational Awards Council, York, 2008.* York: UVAC, pp81–95.

Eyres, R., Hooker, E., and Pringle, A.J. (2008) Engaging with workforce development: what do staff in higher education need?, in Tallantyre, F. (ed.) *Workforce development: Connections, frameworks and processes,* York: Higher Education Academy, pp. 99–110.

Haddleton, F. (2010) Maintaining HE standards in accredited in-company training, in Tallantyre, F., Kettle, J. and Smith, J. (eds.) *Quality and responding to employer needs, York: HEA,* pp27–45.

QAA (2010a) Institutional Audit Harper Adams University College, available at http://www.qaa.ac.uk/reviews/reports/institutional/HarperAdams10/RG617HarperAdams.pdf, accessed 21st April 2011.

QAA (2010b) *Employer-responsive provision survey. A reflective report.* Gloucester: QAA.

Stubbs, W. (2008) The quality assurance of work-based learning and employer engagement' project in *Higher Education Skills in the Workplace Delivering employer-led higher level work-based learning. The abridged proceedings of The University Vocational Awards Council, York, 2008.* York: UVAC, pp30–35.

Whitemore, D. and Minton, A. (2010) Rapid response and fit-for-purpose solutions for HE employer provision, in Tallantyre, F., Kettle, J. and Smith, J. (eds.) *Quality and responding to employer needs, York: HEA, pp118–136.*

CHAPTER 18

Interpreting Academic Level Descriptors for Work Based Learning

Dr Barbara Workman, National Teaching Fellow and Principal Learning Development Consultant, Institute for Work Based Learning, Middlesex University

Angela Maguire, London Region Coordinator, **fdf**

Executive Summary

This chapter outlines the purpose and application of level descriptors currently in use in Higher Education (HE) and vocational learning and how they link to work based learning. It will consider the differing frameworks in use, how academic level descriptors contribute to qualifications and whether different frameworks articulate with each other. The main level descriptors for HE are qualification descriptors compiled by QAA, the Framework for Higher Education Qualifications (FHEQ) and credit level descriptors devised by SEEC (South England Consortium for Credit Accumulation and Transfer). The level descriptors for the vocational sector are those overseen by the Qualifications and Credit Framework (QCF), the Sector Skills Councils (SSC) and National Occupational Standards (NOS). Some differences and similarities between the two approaches will be considered in relation to their characteristics, the benchmarks for subject content or vocational requirements and the implications for size and level of qualifications in relation to appropriate measures.

Background

The recent move to provide employer responsive provision at HE level involves Higher Education Institutions (HEI's), the Quality Assurance Agency (QAA), employers engaged in work force development and Professional and Regulatory bodies such as those involved with Apprenticeships and National Occupational Standards (NOS). The government department Ofqual (the Office of the Qualifications and Examinations Regulator) oversees the Qualifications and Credit Framework (QCF) which is designed to recognise achievement at all levels, starting primarily with vocational qualifications. Each of these bodies offers varying perspectives on level descriptors which are driven by political, occupational or educational agendas. A summary of level descriptors at nine levels from Entry (pre GCSE) to level 8 (Doctorate) are outlined in the National Qualifications Framework (NQF; http://www.ofqual.gov.uk).

Level Descriptors

Level descriptors have been devised for the vocational sector and the higher education sector. They describe the expected outcomes of learning and achievement resulting from a learning activity at any one of the nine levels. These range from level 2, which reflects qualifications at GSCE level; to level 3 at 'A' level or NOS level 3; to level 6 which describes a Bachelor Honours award; level 7 which is Master's-level, and finally level 8 which is doctoral level. This chapter focuses on levels which are used in HE qualifications and higher vocational qualifications.

Level descriptors are used to promote parity of expectation and achievement between different subject or vocational areas. They set consistency of standards and benchmark expected levels of learning and achievement. The achievement level is considered separately from the learning context, the process of learning, the length of time involved or the sequence of study (Lester 2009).

Each level has a range of characteristics related to the complexity of learning activities and assessment expectations for everyone involved (see table 1). These provide a benchmark against which progress can be measured (Greatorex 2003). For vocational subjects the QCF (2010) provides a tariff that states the shared understanding of learning and achievement at each level which are designed to be used across a range of learning contexts. For Higher Education (HE) the Framework for Higher Education Qualifications (FHEQ) (QAA 2008), describes the attributes and outcomes of each HE qualification based on achievement and attainment rather than numbers of years of study. However, for employers and other education providers, it is sometimes helpful to explain the links between levels by describing level 4 as being equivalent to first year undergraduate level, level 5 as second year and so on. This helps learners and employers to have an understanding of levels as related to the workplace.

There are two ways of using level descriptors: either as qualification descriptors such as in the QCF and FEHQ which act as a quality mechanism, or as credit level descriptors as used in NOS units or HE modules which describe the learning outcomes that derive from the qualification level descriptors (SEEC 2010). The macro level relates to the whole qualification and encompasses all qualifications at that level. The micro level consists of modules or units and the credit levels and volumes required to build the qualification.

Level descriptors are generic statements of the intended outcomes of study and outline the types of qualification, the quality and assessment measures required (QAA 2008) and even funding approaches (Lester 2009). Additionally they state the wider abilities that are typically developed as an outcome of a particular level of qualification (QAA2008). For example, the QAA (10/ 2008) qualification descriptors include guidance for HE qualifications to ensure a consistent application of titles for Honours or Foundation Degrees and their expected structure. This ensures a consistent reference point across the HE sector.

Learning Hours

As well as qualitative outcomes, level descriptors may also comprise the length of study in relation to hours of learning. The tariff that is used indicates that 1 credit represents 10 hours of notional learning, with a traditional HE year totalling 120 credits for full time students. For lower level descriptors (levels 1–5 QCF) Guided Learning Hours (GLH) are allocated to an award, usually stating specific learning activities to be precisely accounted for within the allotted time. For higher level descriptors (levels 4–8 FHEQ) it is considered to be notional hours of learning to reflect the average full time students study hours as approximately 35 hours a week. For work-based learners, work time is also considered as learning time, although learning activity also occurs outside the workplace. For part time work based learners, an unrealistic expectation of the amount of study time required can negatively impact the quality and productivity of learning. Consequently recognising and accrediting learning from the workplace should recognise and incorporate learning time at work.

Subject Benchmarks

University courses are informed by subject benchmarks which state the expectations of a named qualification at a given level. For example, this includes the range of subject knowledge and the type of thinking and problem solving skills involved in a given discipline. Engineering, for example, would include mathematical concepts and capabilities required, whereas the humanities would emphasise documentary analysis and written communication. Subject benchmarks offer universities diversity and innovation in programme design as qualifications can reflect local research knowledge but enable equity in level and complexity of study. Work-based learning does not have subject benchmarks, but may use other characteristics to demonstrate parity with traditional qualifications, such as accreditation of local industrial knowledge and practice or Professional standards.

Vocational qualifications recognised by the QCF and National Apprenticeship Service (NAS), or National Occupational Standards (NOS) also set standards for specific awards by specifying the vocational knowledge and skills. These may be quite prescriptive in terms of content, learning expectations and assessment threshold. For example, NOS guide the training expectations in specific sectors to ensure standard levels of practice, competence and quality assurance. The number of credits for qualifications at the lower levels tend to be quite small, and are reflected in the QCF qualifications tariff of recognising Awards (1–12 credits), Certificates (13–36 credits), and Diplomas (37 credits and above). Unfortunately the QCF qualification titles may cause some confusion with employers of professional bodies when discussing similar small HE qualifications. Additionally there may be funding implications for part time learners at level 4 and above. However, higher level qualifications do not have to slavishly follow NOS's, but may interpret the essential vocational knowledge and skills within an HE framework (QCF 2010). Employers and education providers may find such interpretation offers more creative options when designing a vocational qualification.

Level descriptors provide the reference point from which to articulate programme and module learning outcomes. In work-based learning it is important that level descriptors are generic rather than specific to enable application to a range of occupational contexts, professions or vocations. Importantly level descriptors should contribute to the learning process by articulating appropriate expectations and demonstrating achievement rather than stifle innovation and creativity.

Useful Level Descriptor Links

The National Qualifications Framework can be accessed at http://www.ofqual. gov.uk. It provides a summary and comparison of the level descriptors in use in England, Wales and Northern Ireland. Scotland also has it's own level descriptors and these can be found at: http://www.scqf.org.uk. The FHEQ has also been mapped against the European standards to demonstrate parity and equivalence with European qualifications and are stated in the Framework for Qualifications of the European Higher Education Area (FQ-EHEA), also known as the Dublin descriptors. The relationship between the FHEQ and Europe is provided by the QAA at: http://www.qaa.ac.uk.

The FHEQ level descriptors use four characteristics of academic qualifications: knowledge and understanding; cognitive or intellectual skills; key or transferable skills and practical skills. Other Frameworks also break their qualifications into characteristics which are summarised in Table 1.

Credit Level Descriptors

Credit level descriptors take a micro approach to qualification standards by interpreting them at module, rather than award, level. Exemplars have been devised by SEEC (South England Consortium for Credit Accumulation and Transfer, 2010). These are particularly helpful for small, short employer work-based awards as they consider learning attributes of the setting in which the learning occurs and skills for practice. The SEEC credit level descriptors have been used extensively within HEI's to assist in the explication of programmes at module level, both for traditional HE programmes and work-based qualifications.

SEEC (2010) identifies six purposes of credit level descriptors:

- To guide assignment of credit though writing learning outcomes
- For curriculum design
- Assist in setting assessment criteria and setting standards
- To support recognition of prior learning
- To communicate expectations to learners
- For staff development

Credit level descriptors are used to develop curriculum design and qualifications within universities, by being customised for local use. The transparency of learning requirements and assessment expectations means that learners and employers both have a clearer understanding of the success criteria and the intended outcomes in terms of skills and abilities.

SEEC (2010:2) define credit level descriptors as:

> ... 'the level of complexity, relative demand and autonomy expected of a learner on completion of a module or programme of learning. They provide a description of levels of learning through a hierarchy of knowledge and skills. ... [they] are a useful reference point for anyone with responsibility for contextualising and credit-rating learning whether this learning derives from within or without the formal curriculum. Their considered use aids consistency and transparency of expectations and outcomes for all parties: academics, employers, professional bodies and learners'.

SEEC (2010:10) breaks these into in-depth characteristics from which to derive learning outcomes. These include the

- Setting, (including operational context, learner autonomy and responsibility for actions)

- Knowledge and understanding

- Cognitive skills (involving understanding concepts and developing critical thinking problem solving, research and enquiry, synthesis and creativity, analysis and evaluation)

- Performance and practice (the ability to adapt to context, performance, team and organisational working, ethical awareness and application)

- Personal and enabling skills (personal evaluation and development, interpersonal and communication skills)

NOS can be applied within unit requirements to describe the learning outcomes and assessment criteria side by side, making expectations transparent for the employer and learner. Applying these characteristics effectively forms the basis for writing learning outcomes to describe the learning expectations at each level, detailing assessment measures and specifying knowledge or skills required to achieve the level.

Employer-based Training

A current challenge in work based learning is recognising and accrediting employer-based training. Experience suggests that some universities are very uncomfortable with accreditation and prefer to impose their interpretation of what and how learning should happen in the workplace through using validated HE modules. However, recognising learning outside HE by applying level descriptors in a structured and facilitative way can make this less challenging to HE as level descriptors should facilitate comparability between vocational and HE sectors. Universities looking for funding outside the public sector could respond to employers' requests for higher level vocational programmes and may recognise this as an opportunity for a potential income stream. Consequently financial realities may drive acceptance of the QCF descriptors alongside that of the FHEQ as joint programmes are devised.

Such cross sector working might be facilitated by the use of a recent Joint Information Systems Committee (JISC) project. The University of Gloucester developed a co-generative toolkit which was set up to facilitate the co-generation of curricula by academics and employers, with the aim of building vocabulary, tasks, outcome and design. This has identified a confusing use of words at different levels. For example: 'carry out' and 'supervise' are level 6 terms in HE, whereas from an employer's perspective these could be used at level 3. Further examples can be seen at www.pebblepad.co.uk/cogent/.

One challenge presented by work based learning is that the knowledge required at work is different to that from HE and is demonstrated by application to practice, rather than by testing theory. Additionally, within work-based learning FHEQ descriptors may not be fully representative of the type of knowledge and skills expected of a work-based learner. The links between HE knowledge and work based knowledge has been worked on and tested within the foundation degree developments over the past ten years (http://www.direct.gov.uk/en/EducationAndLearning/QualificationsExplained/DG_10039022) As the government agenda of increasing vocational pathways through HE and apprenticeship routes develop, the reluctance by universities to recognise work-based knowledge may gradually subside.

An example of different expectations of qualifications between occupations and HE can be seen in the 'Specification of Apprenticeship Standards for England' (SASE). These include the Higher Apprenticeship Frameworks up to level 5 and state that the apprenticeship must include a competence and technical knowledge qualification, also including national requirements in employee rights and responsibilities; personal learning and thinking skills, and guided learning hours for on and off the job training (BIS 2011). The aim is to extend Higher Apprenticeships up to and including level 6. However, this prescriptive content at higher HE levels may limit the creativity of the learning experience as the HE cognitive skills and theoretical knowledge takes precedence over the competency based skills. Closer working between employers, NOS and HE might help to develop Higher Apprenticeship routes that are less prescriptive, but meet the needs of all involved.

Although the QCF is working to align vocational qualifications with HE there remain some mismatches across levels. For example, agreed NOS competency standards ensure parity of performance by prescribing the type of assessment evidence, which may not include academic skills. NOS are written at job levels, for example first line/middle manager, and not at academic levels, so although they reflect a particular QCF level, they do not necessarily equip the learner with academic skills at the equivalent level of the FHEQ. Evidence of this is when learners complete NOS at level 3, which is an accepted entry to university, but then struggle with the academic learning at level 4 in an FHEQ award. Educational providers, employers and learners need to be aware that different skills are evidenced across the same numerical levels but achievement at one level and context does not necessarily make for smooth transition to another. Consequently academic skills support for learning at HE level should be considered as essential for HE level study, wherever it occurs.

Lessons Learned

This chapter has identified two main approaches and at least five different frameworks in use in the UK; including FHEQ (England, Wales, Northern Ireland and European levels); QCF; SEEC; NOS and SASE. Each is used within different sectors to:

- Set levels of achievement within specific awards

- Guide learning experience and expectations

- Structure and organise programme content and delivery

- Determine the complexity and level of learning activities

- State assessment expectations

- Standardise quality measures

- Promote progression at, and between levels, and allow transfer of learning and credit

- Specify the scope of an award

It is evident that level descriptors differ depending on the particular needs of the sector they represent, although there are commonalities. It would appear that they are evolving to meet the needs of higher level learning between universities and the workplace. There is still room for specific work-based level descriptors to be developed to reduce the mismatches between education and work. Inevitably there is jargon and different understanding of their use which suggests that further interpretation into accessible language is overdue. It begs the question; to what extent are level descriptors working effectively across the vocational and educational divide?

Table 18.1: Summary of Level Descriptor Frameworks and their Characteristics

Title of Level Descriptor framework	Levels covered	Characteristics
FHEQ Framework for Higher Education Qualifications	L 4–8	Knowledge, cognitive skills, learner autonomy, application problem solving, communication, decision making, professional development
QCF Qualifications and Credit Framework	L Entry–8	Knowledge and understanding, application and action, autonomy and accountability
SEEC Southern England Consortium for Credit Accumulation and Transfer	L 3–8	Setting, knowledge and understanding, cognitive skills, performance and practice, personal and enabling skills

Title of Level Descriptor framework	Levels covered	Characteristics
FQ-EHEA (Dublin Descriptors) Framework for qualifications of the European Higher Education Area	L 4–8	Knowledge and understanding, application of knowledge and understanding, Ability to make judgements, ability to communicate, learning skills
NQF National Qualifications Framework	L Entry–8	Qualifications across QCF and FHEQ
SASE Specification of Apprenticeship Standards for England	L2 – Apprenticeships L3 – Advanced Apprenticeships L 4 & 5– Higher Apprenticeships	Qualification Sector skills, including NOS, functional skills, employee rights and responsibilities, personal learning and thinking skills, guided learning hours
Subject Benchmarks	L 6 and some L 7	Achievement at: threshold, typical or excellent intellectual skills, practical skills, numeracy, communication skills, ICT skills, interpersonal and teamwork skills, self-management and professional development skills subject specific knowledge and understanding
NOS	Job level Operational to executive	Standards: skills, knowledge, understanding and behaviours

References

Greatorex J. (2003) Developing and Applying Level Descriptors *Westminster Studies in Education.* Vol 26, (2) 125–133)

Lester S (2009) Issues in defining levels in qualification and credit frameworks http://www.sld.demon.co.uk/levels.pdf accessed 19th May 2011

QAA (2010) *Employer-responsive Provision Survey: A Reflective Report* London QAA

QCF (2010) Guidance for using level descriptors within the qualification and Credit framework Version 4 http://www.paa-uk.org/Qualifications/Regulated/Qualifications/QCF%20Info/QCF%20Support%20Pack/Level%20Descriptors%20in%20the%20QCF.pdf accessed 19th May 2011

SEEC (2010) Credit Level Descriptors for Higher Education SEEC www.seec.org.uk

CHAPTER 19

Speedy Quality Assurance Processes for Fast and Effective Validation and Accreditation of Employer-based Training Programmes

Alison Felce, University Co-ordinator of Work-based Learning, University of Wolverhampton

Cathy Shaw, Deputy Head of Academic Standards and Quality, University of Wolverhampton

Julie Waters, Operations Manager, Avoca Systems Ltd

Executive Summary

The University of Wolverhampton has developed a speedier route for the validation and accreditation of training provided by employers to significantly reduce the time from initial contact from the employer to completion of validation / accreditation. Flexible Learning Opportunities at Wolverhampton (FLOW) is a process through which the university receives and progresses proposals for development and delivery of provision for a CPD market that is both responsive to market demand and ensures oversight of quality assurance and maintenance of standards.

This chapter will present the key aspects of the FLOW process, the reasoning behind its development and the benefits to primary stakeholders. Key principles will be identified to enable others to benefit from the learning and development undertaken by Wolverhampton. A case study of the accreditation of one employer-based training provision is given.

Strategy

The University of Wolverhampton (UoW) has a long history of working with employers, for example through the provision of bespoke training courses as targeted Continuing Professional Development (CPD) activity, master classes (where employer representatives present specialist lectures and seminars) and research partnerships. The University is 'currently ranked first in the United Kingdom for Knowledge Transfer Partnerships' (UoW, 2011). These partnerships, between a business, a graduate and a university subject specialist, are designed and negotiated to help improve business competitiveness, productivity, performance and profitability and for the business to achieve strategic growth. A detailed survey to audit CPD activities with employers was undertaken in 2007 and identified that 'up to 40% of staff engaged' with CPD-type activity with 'costs related to contact days with the community assessed at £5.5 million' (UoW, 2007, in Felce & Purnell, forthcoming). Consequently the University is well placed to work with their existing employer networks to recognise the learning that is currently led by the employer and to identify how this aligns with, and fits into Higher Education (HE), through the nationally recognised Framework for Higher Education Qualifications (QAA, 2001).

External drivers such as the Leitch Report (2006), reports by the Department for Business, Innovation and Skills (BIS, 2009) and by Advantage West Midlands (AWM) and the Learning Skills Councils (LSC), (AWM, 1999, 2007; AWM & LSC, 2008) have identified skills and output gaps within the English West Midlands region and that 'more needs to be done to offer a broader range of models to widen participation; models such as work-based study' (BIS, 2009 in Felce & Purnell, forthcoming). Where employer-led learning can be recognised as equivalent to HE learning employees can achieve HE credits towards an HE award, or an HE award, and access to further HE level studies, for both undergraduate and postgraduate awards.

However, University processes for designing and approving learning have been based on traditional methods of study, for instance full-time and part-time foundation degrees and honours degrees, and they lack the flexibility to respond to external business timeframes. At the University of Wolverhampton we developed the 'FLOW process' (Flexible Learning Opportunities at Wolverhampton) to enable us to respond quickly to assess and quality assure employer-led learning. The FLOW process is complementary to the existing Academic Planning process which continues to apply to the majority of curricula developments across the University.

Process

Overview

The Quality Assurance Agency (QAA) is a government-funded organisation with responsibility for checking how well universities and colleges 'meet their responsibilities, identifying good practice and making recommendations for improvement' and 'publish guidelines to help institutions develop effective systems to ensure students have high quality experiences' (QAA, 2011). The QAA defines CPD as: 'a range of short and long training programmes, some of which have an option of accreditation, which foster the development of employment-related knowledge, skills and understanding.' (QAA, 2010).

The University specifies that FLOW is a process for a range of developments for a CPD market and has identified three initial routes:

1. CPD provision for professions and sector employers

2. Development of small units of study to meet learning needs identified through market research

3. Accreditation of externally delivered provision through:

   a. Direct contact with subject specialists in the Academic Schools

   b. Approaches through the EBTA Community of Practice

   c. Identification of potential client need through market research

Employer-led learning is covered by types '3' a, b, and c and these will be the focus of the remainder of this chapter.

Key to the new process is that it will 'work alongside current quality and validation processes drawing on existing features' (UoW, 2010:1) and that the structure will 'allow the University to be responsive to market demand while providing the key areas that must be adhered with to ensure the University's oversight of activity and arrangements for quality assurance and standards' (UoW, 2010:1). So we are not 'reinventing the wheel' we are reshaping it for a different need.

FLOW panel constituency and remit

A 'FLOW panel' has been set up with its remit to ratify decisions on CPD related provision, to maintain an overview of CPD provision across the University and of employer/partner involvement in its delivery, and to review, evaluate and update the FLOW procedures to assure quality of the CPD delivery. Membership of the panel includes the Head of the Quality Management Division, QMD, (with responsibility for Academic Standards and Quality) and the University Co-ordinator of Work-based

Learning (a strategic role to support curriculum development and initiatives in this area), with representation from the Academic Schools and Services departments as appropriate. The FLOW panel works in conjunction with School Quality Enhancement Committees (SQECs) to achieve recognition or accreditation or validation of employer-led learning. The remit of SQECs is to 'ensure that the School's academic provision (taught, award bearing and non-award bearing) is of high quality and standards and enhances learning and teaching' (UoW, 2011).

Risk Assessment

Across the University curricula a key quality assurance process is the use of a Risk Assessment Tool (RAT), the main purpose of which is to guide the decision makers in the level of scrutiny required. The existing tool has been adapted for FLOW; the RAT for each CPD provision assists the FLOW panel in determining appropriate level of scrutiny during validation, assessing the period of approval and review and the on-going quality assurance monitoring that will be required. The RAT is a four-page template containing fourteen questions against which the proposer ranks the planned CPD provision. The total of the individual 'scores' determine the 'risk' to the University in the arrangement and these are then considered as Low, Medium or High risk proposals. A RAT is completed at the earliest stage possible in negotiations with an employer to ensure that the development team within the School and the employer organisation can be fully supported in the initiative. Once the RAT has been submitted to the FLOW panel, via the SQEC, the CPD provision can be put forward for approval.

Categories of employer-based training

In addition to the RAT, the School must complete and submit an analysis of the external provider provision which summarises the key aspects of the proposal and provides a range of evidence to support the proposal going forward.

The University has identified three sub-categories of employer-led learning that it is likely to be asked to consider, these are identified in FLOW as:

1. **Accreditation of learning delivered by partner**: 'all content is owned by the partner and all assessment is set and conducted by the partner' (UoW, 2010:3)

2. **Completion of partner provision**: all content as in 1 except 'no assessment is included or undertaken' (UoW, 2010:3)

3. **Endorsement of partner provision**: recognition 'that the training is at HE level but no assessment of credits or mapping against and award or module is undertaken' (EBTA in UoW, 2010:3)

Further guidance for the employer and the proposing School on the processes and supporting documentation for each sub-category are also provided.

Partner audit

In common with all other partnerships that the University enters into a 'partner audit' must be undertaken and a Memorandum of Understanding (MoU) or a Memorandum of Co-operation (MoC) must be drawn up. The details of the partnership arrangements determine whether a MoU or MoC is required.

On-going quality assurance and review

The School is responsible for undertaking annual monitoring of the employer-led learning and a regular review of the partnership contract and for reporting this through the standard University procedures.

Outcomes

In its Institutional Audit of the University of Wolverhampton in 2008 the QAA noted that 'confidence can reasonably be placed in the soundness of the institution's present and likely future management of the academic standards of the awards that it offers' and of 'the quality of the learning opportunities available to students'. (QAA, 2008:3)

Cognisant of this external validation of quality assurance within the University the FLOW processes do not amend any of the existing systems, procedures, roles or responsibilities but have been designed to offer an alternative for specified activities that can be completed within a shorter time-frame to better meet the needs of employers seeking recognition for their learning provision whilst still assuring that the quality standards are maintained. Although the time taken for a proposal to be approved will vary, dependent on a number of factors, the FLOW route will typically take no more than 12 to 15 weeks to complete.

The introduction of the FLOW panel has ensured that the University has oversight of the range of CPD type approvals and can work with the Schools to ensure consistency in their partnerships for employer-led learning and that best practice can be identified and shared. Anecdotal evidence suggests that there has been an increase in enquiries for the accreditation of employer-based training. The existence of the FLOW process has enabled the growth of a community of practice within the UoW for those involved in this work.

Case Study

Avoca Systems Limited (Avoca) was established in 1995 and offers data management/migration/informatics services across the healthcare sector. Since its establishment Avoca has developed a 12–18-month training scheme to support its in-house need for high calibre Data Analysts. The programme, the 'Avoca Higher Diploma in Health Informatics' covers five key areas: NHS Knowledge, Informatics Skills, SQL Programming and Database Administration, Project Management and Consultancy Skills and Avoca Data Migration Process. Between 2005 and 2010 67 employees enrolled on the programme. In 2010 EBTA consultants worked with Avoca personnel to commence the process of HE accreditation. The reasons for seeking accreditation were identified as:

- To strengthen the current programme so that Avoca may extend their training provision to external clients

- Provide an accredited training route for new Avoca recruits, and to later extend this to provide a structured training route to support the development of 18 year old school leavers

- To strengthen Avoca's current status as an accredited training centre under the Health Informatics Quality Scheme for learning and development (EBTA, 2010)

The UoW, as a member of the EBTA Community of Practice, was invited to submit an 'Expression of Interest' (EOI) to undertake the accreditation of the Avoca programme. The initial request was received in QMD and the Academic Schools with the relevant subject expertise (the School of Technology, STech, and the School of Health and Well-being, SHaW) were invited to consider the proposal. Once the Avoca programme's fit with existing subject specialisms, Academic School and University strategic plans, was confirmed a small team prepared the first stage of the selection process i.e. completion of the EBTA EOI template. This includes: statement of expertise in the subject area, proposed accreditation, timescale and costs estimate. In addition to the whole programme accreditation requested the UoW also suggested the option of accreditation of identified elements of the programme in 5-credit units and/or 20-credit modules as well as progression routes onto other awards at the University. Avoca invited UoW to the second stage, a presentation and interview at their regional offices, and selected UoW to accredit their programme.

As a small business it was important to Avoca, that the cost structure for the award was flexible. It was clear from the presentation that the University had considered and understood Avoca's needs and that the University were willing to be flexible and adaptable to accommodate these. The offer of further time and consultation to explore the full extent of possibilities at no extra costs helped foster the partnership ethos, and the presenter set out a clear vision for partnership based on subject matter expertise and this inspired Avoca's confidence in the University. The meeting served to demonstrate how closely compatible the University's vision was in helping Avoca achieve its goals, and the significant value the University could add to assist in the further development of training or recouping some of the initial cost on a short term or long term basis, helped create the foundations for a long term partnership.

The accreditation was managed through the FLOW process and comprised the following key activities and stages:

1. Meeting between Avoca course team, UoW subject specialists, UoW QMD and FLOW Panel representatives to agree requirements and deadlines

2. Review of draft costings from EOI and agreement on finalised figures

3. Exchange of Letters of Intent to confirm planned partnership arrangements

4. Review of course documentation, learning materials, and assessment by UoW to confirm HE level and credit. Access to all materials was provided by Avoca to an e-storage site

5. Internal progress meeting at UoW to review activities, QA requirements, reaffirm deadlines

6. Moderation of past student work and collection of data for RAT and Partner Approval, oversight of Avoca QA and student management processes and a UoW visit to Avoca

7. Preparation of RAT, Memorandum of Co-operation, Roles and Responsibilities, NHS Skills Framework Mapping and Accreditation Specification Document by UoW

8. Internal progress and review meeting at UoW to check documentation prior to final approval

9. UoW confirmatory letter of accreditation of the programme

10. Memorandum of Co-operation signed

The Avoca accreditation is one of the first partnerships to be managed through the FLOW process, previously work would have gone through the fuller (and longer) academic development process.

From the employer's perspective, the effort to ensure the training scheme was robust and fit for purpose prior to beginning the accreditation process was time well spent, as once in the FLOW process, input was minimal. The initial meeting with members of the FLOW panel proved an efficient and effective method to discuss the course accreditation and beyond that point queries about the process were dealt with in a speedy and responsive way through telephone and email consultation. Similarly the University NHS Knowledge Skills Framework (NHS KSF) expertise added value to the accreditation process by making it industry relevant for the business.

Overall the employer felt the accreditation was worthwhile and the fact that business timescales were met has inspired confidence to move onto further collaborative work, ensuring the longevity of the partnership is sustained.

Lessons Learned

- Clearly set out processes and procedures and seek approval through the University governance

- Adapt existing processes where possible. Where new processes are required ensure they align with the existing processes

- Direct responsibility for quality assurance and compliance with procedures rests with the Academic School(s) who will manage the partnership arrangements

- Maintain oversight of all proposals at a University level to ensure quality is assured and to identify good practice for dissemination across all provision

- Work with potential partners to agree activities and timeframes and maintain effective channels of communication at all times

References

Advantage West Midlands (1999) *Creating advantage: the West Midlands economic strategy.* Available online at: http://www.advantagewm.co.uk/Images/1999%20-%20WMES%20 Creating%20Advantage_tcm9-13552.pdf (accessed 16th April 2011).

Advantage West Midlands (2007) *West Midlands Economic Strategy: Connecting to Success.* Available online at: http://www.advantagewm.co.uk/Images/WMES_tcm9-9538.pdf (accessed 16th April 2011.

Advantage West Midlands & Learning Skills Council (2008) *Skills Action Plan: West Midlands Region – 2008–2011.* Available online at: http://readingroom.lsc.gov.uk/lsc/WestMidlands/nat-skillsactionplan-mar08.pdf (16th April 2011).

Department for Business Innovation and Skills (2009) *Higher Ambitions: The future of universities in a knowledge economy.* Available online at: http://www.bis.gov.uk/wp-content/uploads/ publications/Higher-Ambitions.pdf (accessed 16th April 2011).

EBTA (2008) *EBTA Guidelines for HEIs v2a: Guidelines to HE providers accrediting employer based training: Quality and Costing Issues.*

EBTA (2010) Consultant's Record Sheets: Avoca Systems Ltd, (Unpublished consultation document, EBTA).

Felce, A. E. & Purnell, E. (forthcoming) Changing policies, their impact on the provision of work-based learning and the development of an e-portfolio based pedagogy for WBL, *Higher Education, Skills and Work-based Learning*.

Leitch, A. (2006) *Prosperity for all in the global economy – world class skills. Final Report (The Leitch Report)*. Available online at: http://www.hm-treasury.gov.uk/media/6/4/leitch_finalreport051206.pdf (accessed 16th April 2011).

Quality Assurance Agency for Higher Education (2011) *About us. Who we are and what we do.* Available online at: http://www.qaa.ac.uk/aboutus/WhatWeDo.asp (accessed 16th April 2011).

Quality Assurance Agency for Higher Education (2010) *Acronyms and glossary of main terms.* Available online at: http://www.qaa.ac.uk/aboutus/acronyms.asp#C (accessed 16th April 2011).

Quality Assurance Agency for Higher Education (2008) *Framework for Higher Education Qualifications in England, Wales and Northern Ireland.* Available online at: http://www.qaa.ac.uk/academicinfrastructure/FHEQ/EWNI08/FHEQ08.pdf (accessed 16th April 2011).

Quality Assurance Agency for Higher Education (2008) *Institutional audit: University of Wolverhampton. November 2008.* Available online at: http://www.qaa.ac.uk/reviews/reports/institutional/Wolverhampton09/RG410Wolverhampton.pdf (accessed 16th April 2011).

University of Wolverhampton (2010) *Flexible learning opportunities at Wolverhampton (FLOW) and the management of CPD proposals.* Available online at: http://www2.wlv.ac.uk/registry/qasd/CPD/Flow.pdf (accessed 16th April 2011).

University of Wolverhampton (2011) *Knowledge Transfer Partnerships (KTP).* Available online at: http://wlv.ac.uk/default.aspx?page=7147 (accessed 16th April 2011).

University of Wolverhampton (2006) *Guidelines for the accreditation of prior learning (APL).* Available online at: http://www.wlv.ac.uk/PDF/aca_apa_guidance.pdf (accessed 7th May 2011).

CHAPTER 20

Approaches to the Recognition of Employer-based Training

Carolyn Hooker, Consultant, People Inclusive

Frances Cambrook, Associate Director, **fdf**

Executive Summary

Many UK universities offer to validate and accredit the programmes of external organisations but few offer endorsement or kite marking, which is referred to here as 'recognition'. Recognition is a form of accreditation but one where there is no credit or award given and although it is a currently underutilised approach it nevertheless represents an option which external partners may welcome if it were to become more widely available. It enables external learning delivery to be recognised and approved by a university to show robustness and quality in HE level delivery. As recognition does not involve the awarding of credit it can also be seen as the first stage for involvement by an organisation with a university, which may then become an opportunity for both to develop an accreditation partnership; in effect recognition may be viewed as the first stage of a developmental process. However, experience indicates that '

> ....to date very few awarding institutions have responded to this demand, possibly because it does not attract HEFCE co-funding.(Haddleton 2010)

In the spring of 2011 research funded by **fdf,** was carried out with a small sample of ten UK universities from the EBTA Community of Practice to collect their experiences and make recommendations to develop this overlooked activity. EBTA had been approached about its knowledge and experience of recognition and wanted an answer to the question of whether, if this had been on offer through EBTA originally, would it have been attractive to employers, as there is a view that employers don't understand credits and they don't want the hassle of assessment.

It is significant that one of the universities reviewed has considerable success in offering recognition and this case study highlights the following:

- How external partners are prepared to seek out recognition and find it valuable

- How recognition can be offered alongside other accreditation activities

- The service can be charged for but a 'lighter touch' is involved compared to full accreditation

- It may become the first stage in a developing partnership

A small number of universities reviewed experimented with recognition and then rejected it and their reasons can be summarised as:

- The approaches made by external partners were often not ones that the universities found attractive and employer engagement staff found that they could not convince senior management of the benefits of a partnership

- Existing processes for handling these requests were similar to full accreditation so the costs were high; alternative approaches were lacking

- There were concerns about reputational risk

Recognition is likely to pose challenges for some universities. However it is important not to reject recognition outright particularly in the current climate as it will be increasingly desirable in the future for universities to become considerably more flexible and employer focused. Activities such as recognition may then offer a more readily available means of broadening the reach of universities in ways in which external partners find attractive and this could lead to increasingly successful engagements that are mutually beneficial.

For the purposes of this review, recognition can be summarised as the following (with acknowledgement to the University of Hertfordshire):

- The quality and standards of the provision are seen as being equivalent to HE generally

- It usually applies to specific provision only (i.e. a particular programme) and not the provider

- There is no credit or award given and no particular HE level is implied

- It is not collaborative provision and no students are registered with the university

- The provider is assessed and rigorously checked by the university

- The provider is allowed to use the university's logo and a form of words which indicates that there is an association (and specifically what this means)

- A formal partnership will be created and reviewed (usually annually)

- The costs involved may be similar to those charged for standard accreditation processes

A University which Recognises the Learning of External Partners

The widely held assumption by universities is that partners will only approach them for programmes for which they would like to receive a qualification, and as this is one of the main functions of universities this has been the dominant mode of engagement. The University of Chester has taken a different approach building on its significant WBL experience, it has an arrangement called 'accreditation' whereby it recognises a small number of organisations' training and development programmes after a process of quality checks and recommended improvements. The scheme is mainly being used for applied and vocational training programmes which are offered outside the normal academic infrastructure but which nevertheless are deemed to have generic HE level equivalence. On completing a prescribed process, the organisation delivering the training is allowed to use Chester's name: 'this programme is accredited by the University of Chester' on their headed note paper. Formal assessment is not normally a requirement on these programmes, by the provider or by the University. The provider will not be requested to deliver anything differently but they are offered advice, which rigorously probes and tests the delivery and the learning outcomes of a programme. As a result of this the University will usually ask that providers accept a number of recommended actions to improve their delivery and they may be asked to follow extra procedures. There have been about eight clients so far who have taken this route and more are expected.

Case Study of The University of Chester, Examples of Organisations and Programmes:

1. An organisation which trains the trainers of sniffer dogs for forensic and drugs work for the police and armed forces. The programme is for handlers working with highly trained dogs and being able to direct them and 'read' their behaviours. It involves an in depth understanding of animal behaviours

2. A company made up of animal behaviourists/scientists who previously worked for a large pharmaceuticals company and then went independent. Again this is animal behavioural work with technicians working with laboratory animals

3. Running family group conferences for family reconciliation which is namely a process of mediation working with the courts and families who are separating through divorce specifically to determine appropriate outcomes for children. In this context the course offers 50% APEL for a post graduate certificate at Chester and is therefore the exception to other programmes so far

4. Personal and business coaching skills. A London company using individual coaching and in-house training and development. The company also works internationally.

Universities Where Recognition is Not Offered

There are universities that have been approached to offer recognition (the University of Hertfordshire and the University of Central Lancashire are two examples) but have declined and their experiences are summarised as follows:

- The third party organisations making the approaches tended to be small and medium sized companies or training providers wishing to enhance their reputations by association

- Some of the provision under consideration would not have been suitable for validation or accreditation because it was modular and 'bite sized', varied in the type of outcomes being achieved and the time involved. Significant changes would have been necessary for any accreditation to have been successful and both the HEI and the company saw this as onerous

- The processes needed to achieve recognition were often very similar to those required for conventional accreditation but the universities became concerned about the absence of future progression for learners

It was believed that in one or two instances better progress would have been made if there had been suitable processes available to deal with recognition and if this had been the case then fruitful and mutually beneficial partnerships could have been embarked upon. However, it was often the case that negotiations were both frowned upon by the university management and rejected due to perceived risks or they floundered early on after becoming 'lost' in finding a suitable way forward.

For the remainder of the universities included in this research, they had either never to their knowledge been approached for kite marking or recognition and they generally regarded it as a high risk activity. Many felt they had other suitable processes already in existence to offer to external partners that were tried and tested which they actively promoted and they had no wish to embark on anything new at this particular time. These processes include Shell frameworks or APEL which are very well established. For example the University of the West of England (UWE) states on its website that 'the framework will act as a shell within which specific pieces of accredited higher learning can be located and accumulated, leading to defined higher education awards'.

Most faculties at UWE now use the Shell framework and the university sees itself very much as the 'partnership university'.

Key Issues and Challenges

Universities have been involved for many years in working with employers through research, knowledge transfer, placements and internships and more recently co-creating and delivering curricula often involving WBL, but the provision of bespoke programmes, the development of very small credit bearing learning opportunities and the accreditation of prior experiential learning is still being explored for its potential. It is very clear that although the existence of employer responsive provision is well established it is nevertheless a relatively small part of a university's activities.

The current challenges for recognition in being more widely accepted as part of this responsiveness are summarised as follows:

- It is perceived as high risk as institutions believe there is no real control over a university's brand

- The lack of approved rigorous and sustainable processes. If processes used for accreditation are the only ones available then the preference of management was strongly in favour of offering these and nothing less

- As implied, the existing accreditation options which are tried and tested are favoured (e.g. Shell frameworks/ CPD awards/APEL)

- There is general uncertainty over the costs that would be incurred and what to charge for these services

- QA considerations and concerns were paramount in a number of cases and how to maintain standards and ensure appropriate outcomes

If recognition continues to be seen as different and requiring a completely separate approach, then again this represents a problem as the common response is 'we're not geared up for anything like that; we don't have the mechanisms'.

1. Concerns of reputational risk

Generally the external organisations that had approached the universities in question (the universities that had decided *against* offering 'recognition') were not well known to them, and they tended to be relatively small or medium sized organisations which the universities genuinely felt did not have a similar reputation to themselves. It is clear that endorsing or 'recognising' provision in this situation would mainly be of benefit to the external organisation and they wanted it primarily for marketing purposes; an association with a university would be used to enhance their reputation but in doing so this carried the risk of diminishing that of the university. A number of approaches were therefore being turned down because the partnership was not welcomed. In a small number of cases this had proved frustrating to the workforce development and business engagement staff of the university as they felt they did know the external organisation and believed that the fears of management were unfounded.

It was also clear that the universities were receiving approaches from interested parties but they themselves were not seeking out partnerships with key organisations/companies who were attractive to them and then considering what they could offer if the potential partner did not want full accreditation. This is a generalisation only being made in this context, as clearly all universities will have working partnerships with a large number of external organisations for a variety of reasons.

When individuals were asked what they thought the outcome might have been if an approach had been made from an organisation which was of a suitable reputation, possibly a large employer well known and respected for its training and development (which may have already been delivering very high quality provision), the answers were somewhat different. It was thought that in this situation if the employer wanted recognition then the request would have been taken more seriously.

Therefore it would appear that concerns of reputational risk are understandably higher in situations in which senior management are approached about external partners of whom they are unsure and that if recognition is seen as enhancing a university's reputation rather than potentially diminishing it, then the final decision may be very different.

2. Uncertainty about processes and procedures

The experience of the majority of universities reviewed was in dealing with the validation and accreditation of assessed programmes, making decisions about learning outcomes and methods of assessment and then taking external programmes through quality assurance processes. This would normally involve full academic scrutiny, formal planning meetings, the production of the relevant documentation, the convening of an approvals panel, written reports, conditions to be met and then validation with the subsequent credit being agreed (in addition to any quality enhancement advice which may have preceded this). Costs for this vary from one university to another but they are often fairly considerable and may include an upfront fee followed by a student related element.

It was largely believed that employers and other partners are only willing to pay these costs when they achieve accredited qualifications and there was widespread concern that recognition might cost the same but deliver a less robust outcome. Starting from a premise of not reducing any processes or costs, respondents were very quick to query who might pay for such a service and why.

3. Absence of a market

The majority of respondents strongly believed there was no market for recognition. If a respondent believed that the costs were likely to be the same as for conventional accreditation processes and the risks were greater, then there were very few reasons to consider pursuing it as an option or in making it available to external partners. Some of the respondents had never been approached for such a service but others who had nevertheless found it impossible to find a way to make it work in their HEIs.

Despite this there was a small minority of respondents (three) who were more optimistic and who were prepared to speculate that firstly costs could be reduced or minimised, that partners of sufficient standing would come forward and be attractive to the university and also that strategic change in the HE sector might also demand a more forward thinking and creative approach. They were also willing to entertain the idea that recognition might prove to be the opening for a number of ventures which would encourage new partners to come onto the 'first rung' of the accreditation ladder, and that this could then develop into mutually beneficial relationships leading to credit bearing programmes.

4. An example of a programme from outside the sector

The final question which needs to be asked, and which cannot be answered by this review is, 'is there a market for recognition and what would it look like'? The missing part of the picture here is what external partners might be prepared to purchase if recognition were widely on offer. There is some market knowledge in this respect but it lies outside the HE sector and with professional institutes, for example the Institute of Leadership and Management (ILM) which runs an endorsement scheme for training providers who deliver leadership and management programmes. Providers can either be 'recognised' as offering a 'Development

Programme' (where learners are not assessed) or an 'Endorsed Programme' (which has assessment). Both types of programme are separate to Approved Centres which offer ILM qualifications, but they are allowed to use an ILM logo which shows that they are either 'recognised' or 'endorsed'. The scheme is not expensive and often leads to wider partnerships.

Lessons Learned

- For most HEIs in this study there are issues and challenges to be faced in offering recognition, but these have been overcome by one institution and there is interest from others to do the same. There has been very little attempt to create demand or generate a special market (and so opportunities may have been missed). It would appear that many HEIs have been mainly reactive rather than proactive and consequently have been approached by private training providers and SMEs who have been unable to persuade them to risk their reputations or make the time and investment to share their brand. On a number of occasions HEIs said that they would think otherwise if they themselves were seeking high status partners with whom they wished to forge an on-going partnership

- Against this backdrop is also the finding that some employer engagement individuals in HEIs experience the current situation as very frustrating. They believe they could be more entrepreneurial and strategic in the market but their senior management are risk averse and inward rather than outward looking. This creates a major disconnect between the employer engagement staff and any access they have to the HEI developing its brand and marketing

- The EBTA initiative was originally created to stimulate demand from employers and to give them an accessible route into HEIs, and it has very successfully created a market for institutions. At the moment there is much uncertainty in the HE sector regarding future funding scenarios but it is likely that the widening participation, employer engagement and the employability agendas will become increasingly important and may prompt HEIs to seriously seek out other routes to market beyond the existing conventional ones.

This report therefore raises the following questions:

1. Are there opportunities which are not being fully exploited by HEIs?

2. What connections can be made between employers and HEIs to mutual advantage which do not demand full accreditation?

3. Which are the partnerships that could enhance HEIs' reputations?

4. What types of proposals would be welcomed rather than rejected? (This may well be specific to an individual HEI.)

5. How can HEIs make more use of their employer engagement resources to really exploit their brands and develop new, sustainable markets?

These questions may be answered by more research and discussion and the approval of processes which encourage action.

References

Haddleton, F. (2010) *Maintaining HE Standards in in-company accredited training*, York: Higher Education Academy

CHAPTER 21

Issues, Challenges and Joys of Accreditation

Celia Moran, Director of Escalate, University of Bradford

Tony Wall, Senior Lecturer and Principal Investigator, Centre for Work Related Studies, University of Chester

Executive Summary

This chapter takes both a strategic and operational view of issues, challenges and joys of accreditation, drawing upon the contributions in this book and the experience of the Escalate Employer Engagement Programme at the University of Bradford. It uses various lessons arising from general engagements with the Employer-based Training Accreditation (EBTA) process and other case studies, as a basis of the analysis and discussion. The observations and conclusions drawn here are broadly applicable to all forms of employer and university partnerships, and not just for the accreditation of training. Like other chapters in this publication, it focuses on the experience of one particular university (in this case University of Bradford), but the chapter also attempts to draw comparisons from across the publication.

The chapter has four main themes:

- The 'strategic imperative' as a prerequisite for embarking upon accreditation

- The 'accreditation maze'. Operationally, accreditation requires a detailed understanding of how a university works, and an ability to navigate through what seems to many, a complex and inaccessible infrastructure. This section identifies the various stages of the EBTA process from the university's perspective and highlights some of the solutions that contributors have developed.

- People and relationships. Ultimately accreditation is about a relationship between the university and an organisation (and in some cases, clusters of them). So not only do colleagues engaging in this activity need a skill set that includes a working knowledge of higher education systems, processes and funding, but they also need 'business facing' attitudes and behaviours that will enable them to communicate with, respond to, and gain the confidence of, organisational partners (and particularly employers). This section explores the issues and lessons learned in brokering relationships between academic colleagues and organisations and identifies ways of building capacity to make it work.

- 'The benefits' This section celebrates some of the success stories that demonstrate that accreditation can bring considerable benefit to employers, learners and universities.

The 'Strategic Imperative'

Successful accreditation involves almost all university services, and without strategic commitment there is no leverage to encourage either academic departments or central services to cooperate. In particular, there are challenges associated with established cultures and ways of working, as well as with competing priorities, which require leadership from the top. As reported by Bolden et al (2009) and noted by Haddleton and Minton (Chapter 16) in their exposition of the first of their 3 Ps for employer engagement 'high level support at VC/DVC/PVC/Dean level is essential, so that key decision makers can influence the wider university systems'.

The Escalate Programme at University of Bradford was conceived from the very start as a strategic cultural change programme, with the aim of changing the University's relationship with business and the local and regional economy. In an earlier account of the Escalate approach, Layer et al (2010) emphasised the importance of ownership and management of the change process by senior colleagues and the organisational governance and management processes that support this.

At Bradford, strategic influence was achieved in a large part through:

1. Deputy Vice Chancellor (Academic), as 'sponsor' of Escalate and Chair of the Programme Board

2. Director of Escalate, as member of key strategic University committees

This enabled important policy changes to be initiated quickly, and also for employer engagement considerations to be factored in to other policy and decision making processes. This is also the experience at other institutions, such as at the University of Chester. In Chester's case, strategic influence is integral to, and embedded within approval processes, by the inclusion of a Pro Vice Chancellor on relevant committees.

The Escalate Business Plan referred to the Bradford challenge as requiring a 'paradigm shift', a major internal cultural change programme, especially in some parts of the University, which would provide the conditions to engage much more effectively with the business world. For Bradford, this was not just about providing a workforce development solution, the idea was to use Escalate to 'flex' central systems and processes and create a responsive and adaptable academic infrastructure that would enable *all* parts of the University to respond effectively to employer requirements, and so would engage all of the University's six Academic Schools as well as its central services.

None of this was ever going to be easy, and as Escalate unfolded, it became apparent that the strategic intervention would need not only to follow through on original commitments and intentions, but would also need to adapt to changing circumstances and the response (or lack of) in some parts of the University. As an example, the original plan to have 'Escalate Champions' in each Academic School had mixed success and so the Escalate Programme Board made the decision to support the appointment of Associate Deans (Employer Engagement) who would exercise strategic influence and leadership of employer engagement within their schools, as well as work at a senior level network to share experience and pursue cross-university opportunities. The DVC (Academic) was pivotal in taking this proposal through the necessary University processes and ultimately securing the approval of Senate.

The 'Accreditation Maze'

A particular challenge associated with accreditation is that it touches almost all of the university's systems and procedures, especially when the accreditation involves making an award. As such it requires considerable higher education experience and detailed understanding of how a university works. For less experienced colleagues the questions and barriers can seem insurmountable.

Academic Infrastructure

Having established the employer's motivation and requirements in relation to accreditation, the first step in the process is to establish that the training can be translated into a programme that is recognisable as higher education and therefore worthy of accreditation, and if so, to determine the academic level and volume of the programme with reference to the academic infrastructure. Many contributors to this publication have referred to the issues and processes involved in this. Haddleton and Minton(Chapter 16) go into some detail stating that these are 'the realm of the academic and it is important that those involved in the discussion with the employers are able to explain [these academic requirements]'

The employer's training programme needs to contain what would be regarded as academic content in a higher education context, where appropriate, referenced to the relevant subject benchmark. It must lead to academic outcomes that can be aligned with the Framework for Higher Education Qualifications (FHEQ), and the volume of learning must be quantifiable so as to assign a credit rating. This in itself can prove something of a challenge when employer training courses tend to focus on 'input' or 'contact', rather than total notional learning hours.

Figure 21.1: Mapping to the Academic Infrastructure

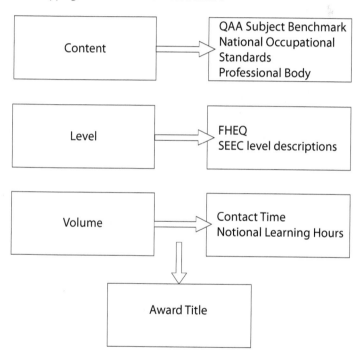

Bolden (as cited by Haddleton and Minton in Chapter 18) highlights the important role of the academic in ensuring that the programme remains fit for purpose for the employer, whilst satisfying the requirements of the academic infrastructure. What is also vital is for this lead academic to act as an 'interpreter' between the employer and the HE institution so that this can be achieved without damaging the relationship What this implies is the need for an experienced academic with strong business acumen.

This 'mapping' of the employer's training programme to the academic infrastructure is described and illustrated by several of the contributions to this publication. In general terms, the process generates learning outcomes for modules, levels and/ or programmes which, if expressed carefully, can ideally be recognised by both the university and the employer (see the Croda Case Study, Chapter 4). The issue of level is addressed in some detail by Workman and Maguire (Chapter 18) on 're-interpreting academic level descriptors for work based learning. As described by Pearson and Helyer (Chapter 14) by factoring in 'volume', a credit value is generated, which if sufficient can lead to a higher education award. The FHEQ includes a relatively limited number of awards, for what many employers would consider a large volume of learning. Many universities have sought to address this matter for their employer responsive provision by developing additional awards which are not part of the FHEQ, but nevertheless provide recognition of achievement for shorter programmes of study.

The University of Bradford, like several other institutions (Willis 2008, Whitemore and Minton 2010), has developed a 'Shell' award framework to facilitate this mapping process, and enable a more streamlined approach to programme approval. This framework expresses the learning in generic terms and provides a robust yet more responsive process for the accreditation of tailored or bespoke programmes within agreed parameters and delegated authority. For Bradford, the development of the principals underpinning the Shell framework for work based learning has been useful in thinking through how this might be adapted and used to develop shell frameworks for other types of provision. The University of Bradford has used its Shell framework in the accreditation of the 'Winning Managers' programme (Chapter 13) and Chapter 3 explains how the University of Gloucestershire used its flexible Shell qualifications framework to accredit the Cathedrals Workforce Fellowship programme. In the description of the University of Chester's work with Learning to Inspire (Chapter 8), Wall, Douglas and Lord conclude that a negotiated flexible learning framework enables the university to work flexibly with a training provider – to swiftly develop new provision according to the needs of the training provider and their clients'. The University of Chester uses its own flexible framework as the standard, de facto, route for employer responsive provision (also see Chapter 7).

A further issue in relation to the academic infrastructure is the evidencing of learning or, as universities would see it, assessment. The challenge here is to develop an assessment strategy that satisfies the requirements of higher education in terms of demonstrating the attainment of learning outcomes in a way that can be externally examined, while adding value in the work place. The assessment needs to be relevant, rigorous and founded in real work activity (Boud and Solomon 2001, cited by Minton and Haddleton, Chapter 16). Any assessment strategy that is seen as an additional burden, or not relevant to the work place, is likely to create a barrier for the employer and/or the employee-learner. In the chapter *Delivering and Evidencing Business Impact Through Higher Level Skills* (Chapter 14) Pearson and Helyer discuss the assessment issue in some detail and explores the ways in which tools that have been developed to measure return on investment can be used to inform and assessment design that meets the needs of all stakeholders.

Pricing

The development and delivery of traditional full-time higher education programmes takes place within a regulated fee regime and as such few academics have experience of costing and pricing their offer, let alone discussing and negotiating a price with a prospective 'client'. The challenge associated with this aspect of accreditation is highlighted by McGregor Brown, whose experience in implementing the EBTA process in West Yorkshire mirrored that of the core **fdf** EBTA team 'the prices quoted ...ranged dramatically...and often even the lowest prices were seen initially by businesses as being too high'. McGregor-Brown and Beaumont (Chapter 15) offer two explanations: firstly that of 'on-costs', and secondly, an unrealistic expectation of 'public sector' prices'. During the very early phases of EBTA, feedback from Community of Practice members indicated that, with notable exceptions, many had no institutional methodology for establishing either cost or price. In these cases colleagues were either operating in the dark, or using 'traditional' approaches based upon established fee and overhead regimes. As part of the Escalate employer engagement programme, a considerable amount of development work was done with the University's management accountants to understand both start-up and recurrent costs associated with accreditation, and then to use this as a way of informing price. The methodology that was developed provided a 'toolkit' to calculate costs, but then allowed flexibility (for example at School level) in determining price.

Employers as Collaborative Partners

Minton and Fenwick (Chapter 4) describe how the University of Derby's relationship with Croda falls within the QAA definition of collaborative provision (QAA, 2010): such cases require approval mechanisms for the delivery by the employer or training provider. Derby has adopted what are referred to as robust yet proportionate processes and documentation that can be completed within a business timeframe. At Bradford, a review of collaborative provision procedures initiated by the Deputy Vice Chancellor (Academic) took into account, among other factors, the experience of using traditional processes for the approval of employer partners and concluded that there was scope for streamlining, clarification and support. A new Academic Partnerships Committee was established to take on the remit of partner approval, and an Academic

Partnerships Office to support and oversee partnership development and review. A central consideration here was to ensure that the University maintains central strategic oversight of its partnerships, and the management of its relationships. The importance of these factors are illustrated in the Booths case study (Chapter 2) which emphasises the need for strategic alignment including shared goals, a shared philosophy, and the benefits of building a strong collaborative working relationship.

Having completed the requisite collaborative provision procedures, the partnership then needs to be formalised and documented in a contract. As with other aspects of the accreditation process, standard templates that have been developed for overseas or further education partnerships often present a problem. Escalate has worked with the University of Bradford's legal team to redesign and/or adapt standard contracts to match the more novel arrangements associated with accreditation, and to develop formats that reflect a 'partnership of equals' and appropriately balance risk management with lightness of touch.

Quality Assurance

Inappropriate, bureaucratic and lengthy quality assurance processes are frequently cited as a barrier to effective and responsive employer engagement, However, as contributors to this publication have reiterated throughout, it is vital training that is accredited by an HEI is recognisable as higher education and has the same rigorous scrutiny and standards applied to it as any other provision. It is this assurance of quality and standards that employers are looking for in accreditation.

The purpose of quality assurance is to safeguard academic standards and this publication clearly demonstrates that is it is possible to do this and to respond to employer requirements. In developing its employer responsive provision, Harper Adams University College has developed what is referred to as 'proportionate' approach to quality assurance (Chapter 17). Their approach ensures the appropriate involvement of employers but recognises that HEIs must retain responsibility for their own robust quality assurance processes. They have developed a template to capture and frame partnership discussions and assist with the assessment of reputational, quality and financial risks. A monthly validation panel meeting which includes external and industry representatives ensures rapid turnaround of this type of provision.

Harper Adams has also adapted traditional external examiner and annual review process for its employer related provision, ensuring that is fit for purpose, bearing in mind its work-related focus. External professional reviewer and professional advisors complement the external examiner system and provide feedback both from learners and on the currency of the curriculum from an employer perspective. Feedback from other key stakeholders is also a feature of annual review and members of staff are encouraged to use different methods of data collection according to the scale and context of the programme. Arnold, Warr and Cowap (Chapter 17) advocate a specialised infrastructure that complements the existing as a way to build organisational capacity and ensure that employer responsive provision is thoroughly scrutinised and understood. Such an approach also facilitates a timely response and a professional approach to relationship management.

Flexible Learning Opportunities at Wolverhampton (FLOW) similarly adapts existing procedures to respond to market demand whilst retaining oversight and ensuring the rigour of academic quality processes (see Chapter 19). FLOW is effectively a risk-based system of delegation to Schools for CPD, accreditation and other provision involving employers which includes clear processes and templates, and typically takes no more than 12 to 15 weeks to complete.

People and Relationships

'People' is the first and probably the most important of Minton and Haddleton's 3 Ps for Employer Engagement. Whatever the processes and the practice, it is ultimately people that make it happen or not. For institutions such as Bradford, that have taken a whole institution cultural change approach to employer engagement, the people dimension extends to all parts of the organisation. In this case, customer responsiveness and business acumen cannot just be the purview of the few, it has to be embedded throughout all external facing and internal 'service' departments so that the whole 'supply chain' can operate in a timely and responsive manner. A single document held on one person's desk, an unnecessary bureaucratic hurdle, or an unprofessional or overly 'academic' conversation can easily damage a valuable business relationship.

Minton and Haddleton (Chapter 16) talk about the importance of employing academics who are comfortable and familiar with working with employers (and organisations outside of higher education) and the importance of valuing and recognising this type of work alongside other forms of teaching and research. Navigating the 'accreditation maze' requires experienced and professional academics. Harper Adams (Chapter 17) involve internal work based learning experts early in the design process as a way to help safeguard standards and Cambrook and Lyddon (Chapter 3) highlight the role of the EBTA consultant as 'mediator', quality assurance 'link tutor, and employer advisor. This role requires a broad and different skill-set to the average academic, but one which in future HEIs will have to provide themselves. Wall and Grant, in their LeaderShape case study (Chapter 7) emphasise the need to work closely, openly and regularly to meet the needs of, and appropriately challenge, well qualified, highly experienced professionals and the importance of listening and adapting.

Staff development is one obvious way to build institutional capacity and develop a skill set appropriate to the accreditation challenge in both their own, and partner, institutions. Escalate has, from the outset, run a series of 'Practice Workshops' for colleagues, sometimes with partners such as West Yorkshire Lifelong Learning Network (WYLLN), **fdf** and EBTA. Harper Adams has built teaching capacity in partner organisations using a 'Training HE trainers' module and invited partners to join learning and teaching events at the College.

The Benefits

The case studies in this book and the record of the EBTA service are both testimony to the potential of higher education accreditation to add value to employer-based training and to bring tangible business benefits. For Booths (Chapter 2), the MMU Foundation Degree in Retail is of strategic significance in supporting the culture of the organisation, and their approach to the development of its retail managers. The strength of the relationship is evident in the platforms that the partners share and in Booth's support for the EBTA service. Strategic alignment is similarly evident in the successful partnership between the Halifax Bank and Middlesex University, an example that illustrates how learning and development can be used to develop desired behaviours and contribute to business improvement. Hull College have assisted P&O Ferries in addressing issues of low staff morale, high turnover and poor performance and University of Leicester's ROI work with DeBeers' Diamond Professional Programme demonstrates that such development can drive performance improvements. The University of Chester's engagement with two training organisations (Chapters 7 and 8) have led to mutual growth. Together, what these and other contributors demonstrate is:

- There are significant benefits to those involved in accreditation. For employers, there are intangible benefits to morale and motivation, and 'bottom line' measurable impacts. For universities, accreditation offers opportunities to expand their reach, connect with new learners, and grow even in times of austerity For the people most central to this, the learner, new opportunities for professional learning and recognition can be created. These benefits can also reach in to industries and communities in a way, distinctive from and largely untouched by traditional higher education approaches

- These benefits can realistically be achieved by a real variety of universities (large, small, research intensive, teaching-focused, for example), and each perhaps with a different model which is suitable for their context. It may be a module, a course, a programme, a department, or a whole university approach

- The commonality across all of these models is the real commitment to quality which is a key 'added value' of accreditation. This includes quality assurance, quality enhancement and quality risk management, all of which may be seen as the complex 'wiring' to those outside of higher education. Though an essential part of university life, there are tried and tested ways to make these processes simpler, more effective, more efficient, and hence create a greater 'fitness fur purpose'

- Working towards this greater 'fitness for purpose', in turn to achieve the wider benefits for all stakeholders, it is essential to have the drive, commitment and capability of university staff to engage and sustain the engagement of professionals working in organisations outside of education. This book uniquely shares the experiences, and learning from work, of such individuals, with a view to encourage, stimulate and develop other individuals and organisations to engage in the same journey. This will create a greater level of impact as the future of higher education becomes more uncertain.

Possible Futures

Within this book we have highlighted partnerships that have led to organisations and universities positively changing the way they do business. Most of them have been established under favourable economic conditions, but some have had to respond to a new climate of austerity (Chapters 6 and 7). It is important, looking forward, to consider these economic conditions, as they are expected to change the landscape in which the above cases have been presented. What can we reasonably expect to happen? And what could the implications of those things be?

The economy is expected to struggle for a number of years, impacting organisations across industries, and particularly in higher education. Higher education has already started to prepare for cuts of 80% to their teaching budgets, including closing down departments who are not profitable or who do not attract students. More universities than the Government expected are charging the full £9,000 annual tuition fee, and so effective demand is expected to fall. Powerful market forces are expected to 'shake out' some of the 'less desirable' universities through closure or merger to rebalance demand with supply. This is clearly a simplification, but works on the priority of most universities being the full time, 18–21 year old 'traditional' undergraduate market. So what can be done?

History consistently demonstrates that in times of such austerity and difficulty, human creativity and ingenuity create new opportunities for growth (notice the current retail growth for big name stores in the UK). Part of the 'shake out' mentioned above will not just be due to popularity and efficiency but also a test of a university's capacity for agility and innovation. Using the models described in this book universities will create, develop and penetrate new markets, creating new income streams for their own future sustainability. We know that more universities are adopting these models, as some of the editors continue to act as national consultants in this capacity. Yet universities will need to do two things to be successful. First, they will need to become *excellent* at it, as customers are not only paying for it there will be alternatives to choose from, and second, they will need to be *swift and agile* at doing it consistently. There is very little time to be investing in innovative approaches before the effects of the 'shake out' hits.

Within these innovations and market forces, Wall (2011) refers to the growth of 'proactive, distributed learning networks' as a growing opportunity. Here, he refers to the growth of 'shell' frameworks in the UK, whereby learners/employers can negotiate the content of their learning journey, leading to a university qualification. Within these frameworks, learning from 'outside' the university, specifically including the sort mentioned throughout this book can be brought together into an award that is pertinent to the individual in their circumstances. In this way, he argues, people can travel through different jobs or roles, and accumulate the professional learning they need, as they need it. In essence, it is *a network of learning journeys, distributed across time and space.* As in this book, those facilitating the journey (such as employers or training organisations) may be designing it, delivering it and assessing it so *they* have a greater ownership over it, and have a vested interest in *making it work* because they are paying for it (in the case of the employer), or are charging for it (in the case of the training organisation). Wall argues, because there is greater ownership and vested interest in making it work, this could be more sustainable model to reach a greater diversity of learning situations. Wall (2011) suggests this model is beginning to grow in various regions in the UK, and that this might be stimulated by the current economic climate. What appears to be important, as mentioned above, is that it takes more than Deans, Pro-Vice Chancellors or Vice Chancellors to make this happen. It can impact everyone involved in the delivery of higher education, registry, admissions, marketing, academic development, research and enterprise teams (Wall, 2010a, 2010b).

What is being evidenced here is a different type of higher education, one which is responsive, flexible and 'fit for purpose'.

References

Boud, D. and Solomon, N. (2001), *Work Based Learning: A New Higher Education?* Buckingham: SRHE and Open University Press.

Bolden, R., Connor, H., Duquemin, A., Hirsh. W, and Petrov, G. (2009) *Employer Engagement with Higher Education, Defining, Sustaining and Supporting Higher Skills Provision,* London CIHE.

Layer, G, Moran, C and Srivastava A, (2010) 'Centralised or devolved structures for managing employer engagement' in Tallantyre, F(ed) (2010) *University Management of Work-Based Learning,* York, Higher Education Academy.

QAA (2010) *Code of Practice for the Assurance of Academic Quality and Standards in Higher Education. Section 2: Collaborative provision and flexible and distributed learning (including e-learning)* – Amplified version October 2010. Available at

http://www.qaa.ac.uk/academicinfrastructure/codeofpractice/section2/collab2010.pdf (accessed .13/05/11)

Wall, T. (2010a) Enabling and disabling discourses in promoting RPLO policy and practice in Higher Education, *Education-Line*, pp1–11.

Wall, T. (2010b) University Models for Validating Work Based Learning, in Roodhouse, S. and Mumford, J. (Eds.) *Understanding Work Based Learning,* London: Gower.

Wall, T. (2011) *Diversity through Negotiation*, in J. Shaw et al (Eds) Student Diversity and Inclusion in Higher Education (working title) (Libri).

Whitemore, D. and Minton, A. (2010) A Rapid Response and Fit For Purpose Solutions for Employers, Which Maintains Standards, York, Higher Education Academy.

Willis, K. (2008), Frameworks for Work-based Learning in Tallantyre, F (ed) (2008) Workforce development: Connections, Frameworks and Processes, York, Higher Education Academy.

Glossary of Terms

Accreditation of Prior Experiential Learning (APEL)	This is the process by which an individual learner can obtain academic credits for learning developed from experiences at work or in professional practice. The university assesses the learning by comparing it with similar learning that might have taken place on campus.
Accreditation of Prior Learning (APL)	This is the process by which an individual learner can obtain academic credits for learning achieved on formal courses and training (e.g. a HND counting towards a BA degree).
Admissions	The university department that takes enquiries from potential students, receives applications and processes these.
Blended Learning	A mode of study made popular by the Open University where learners mostly study at a distance, but with some campus sessions and some online learning. The balance between these can vary, and sometimes can be negotiated with your tutor.
Board of Studies	Official body in each university where teachers and learners discuss the concerns of learners and make a record of these for action to be taken. It is an important forum for the learner voice to be heard. All academics must demonstrate they listen to, and take action to address concerns raised at Board of Studies.
Credits and Credit Points	University qualifications are made up of specific amounts of credits. You need to complete the specified number of credits to achieve a particular qualification. So for example, to gain a Bachelors degree with honours (BA Hons) you need to successfully complete 360 credits. Credits in higher education can be transferred between universities.
Distance Learning	A mode of study where you do not attend the university for 'lectures' but where the 'learning' and the 'teaching' are run in separate locations. Your tutor may be in her office at the university while you undertake your studies at home or in the workplace. Distance learners usually have learning materials specifically designed for this mode of study.
Enrolment	The process by which you agree to take the place on the programme and accept the responsibility to pay any fees.
Formative Assessment	This is where a tutor assesses a learner's performance or work to provide feedback on how improvements can be made. It is usually undertaken at points during the course of a module or unit.

Higher Education	This is the highest level of education available provided by special institutions that are either universities, university colleges or other specialist centres that deliver higher education. The term is interchangeable with 'university-level'.
Higher Education Institution (HEI)	A university, university college or other institution that has been granted the right to make UK Higher Education Awards by the Privy Council.
Induction	The process by which the university introduces you to its systems, regulations and support available to you as a learner. This is often campus based, but may be virtual or through documents sent to you by post.
Learning Materials	Handbooks and study materials given to you so you can follow a particular module or unit. This might include a Reader (see Reader) and a list of suggested reading.
Learning Resources	The term used to describe university services that support learning. These will include library services, email and access to the university network. Can also include placement services, careers advice etc.
Mode of Study	Universities deliver their programmes in significantly different 'modes' which include 'full time'; 'part time'; 'on campus', 'flexible learning'; 'distance learning'. This may have greater importance to the university and their funding arrangements than your experience as a learner. It may have fee and funding implications for you.
Modules or Units	The parts that make up a university qualification. They are usually followed in a specific sequence towards a specific qualification title. There may be 'core' modules / units which you must successfully complete, and 'optional' modules / units which you can choose from as part of your programme.
National Qualifications Framework	The list of academic and vocational qualifications and an attempt to indicate the equivalence between vocational and academic qualifications.
NVQ	National Vocational Qualifications (NVQs) are work-related, competency-based qualifications. They do not reflect the higher level learning skills of higher education, but place emphasis on specific skills and knowledge for particular jobs.
Negotiated Modules or Units	Modules or Units where the focus of the studies is negotiated between you, the university, and often your employer (if applicable).
Online Learning	A university programme run entirely using a web-based system.
Programme / Programme of Study	The series of modules you undertake in order to reach your target qualification. The programme may include, or be made up entirely of negotiated modules / units.
Programme Leader	Member of academic staff with responsibility for leading the delivery of a whole WBL or traditional programme at undergraduate or postgraduate level.

Qualifications	These are 'certificated' awards made by universities, colleges and professional training organisations. University qualifications have a range of titles that are usually linked to the academic level.
Reader	A handbook with extracts from books and other literature which you are expected to read and use as part of a module or unit.
Registration	The process by which you apply to become a learner at university. This means making an application for a programme of study, course or module. After sending in an application form, you are likely to be asked to sign a letter confirming you would like to accept the place on the programme.
Registry	The university department which holds the information on learners, the programmes they are following, their grades, and their final award.
Semesters / Terms	Most universities organise teaching into two semesters or three terms per year. Each is followed by a period in which official assessment of learners' work is undertaken. Semesters run late September to end of December and late January to mid May. Terms normally run in the Autumn, Winter and Spring, as in schools.
Summative Assessment	This is where a tutor (and sometimes the workplace) assesses a learner's performance or work to grade it. It is usually undertaken at the end of a module or unit and 'sums up' achievement. You will normally receive feedback to help you understand how the grading has been made.
Tutor	The tutor is the academic who runs the modules you are taking as part of your course. They may also be known as: Programme Adviser, Academic Advisor, Academic Supervisor etc.
Tutorial	One to one or small group meeting with a university tutor. It may be in person, by telephone, video-link or online.
University-level	A term that is usually applied to qualifications and learning. Qualifications are graduate level (i.e. from graduate certificate to doctorate). When applied to learning, the term means learning of the highest level of complexity, breadth and detail.
VLE / Virtual Learning Environment	All universities have 'Virtual Learning Environments' which learners can access to support their studies. They will often have handbooks and other materials online. They can be accessed from any computer with web access. VLEs may also have specific tasks for you to undertake as part of your module or unit, and include blogs or other methods of communication between learners. You normally need to be a registered and enrolled learner to access these services.
Worker Researcher / Insider Researcher	A very important concept in WBL which recognises the importance of the WBL learner as both a worker and researcher. Its main importance is in relation to ethical dilemmas that might arise, and the relevance of knowledge the learner may develop in the workplace or professional setting.

Index